CAMRA'S
Lake District
Pub Walks

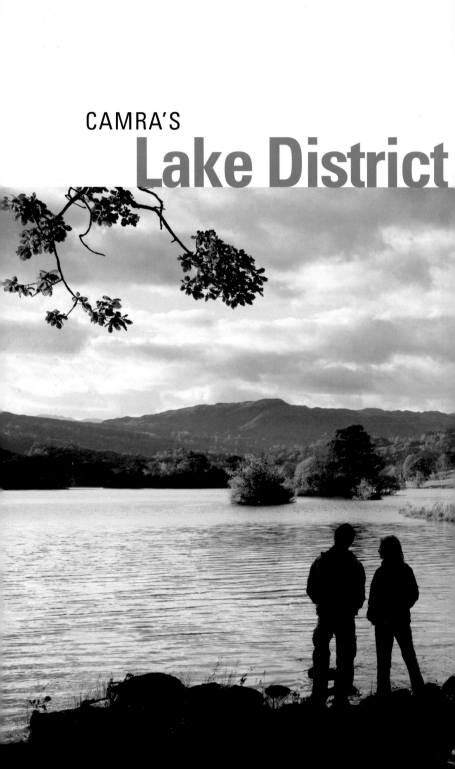

CAMRA'S
Lake District

Pub Walks

BOB STEEL

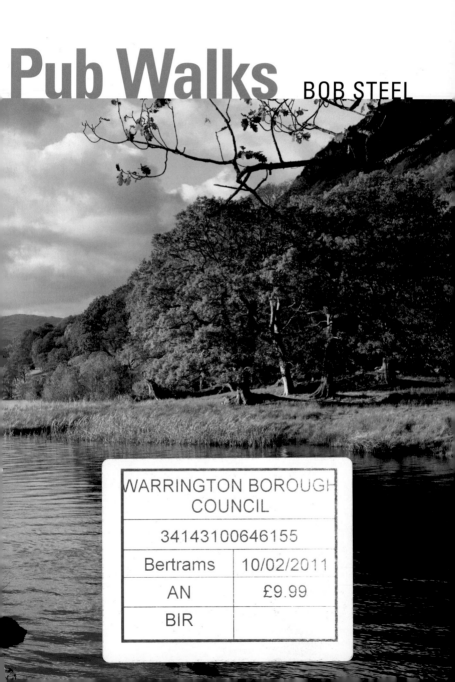

Published by the Campaign for Real Ale Ltd.

230 Hatfield Road
St Albans
Hertfordshire AL1 4LW
www.camra.org.uk/books

Design and layout © Campaign for Real Ale Ltd. 2011
Text © Bob Steel

ISBN 978-1-85249-271-7

A CIP catalogue record for this book is available
from the British Library

Printed and bound in China by Latitude Press Ltd

Head of Publishing: Simon Hall
Project Editor: Katie Hunt
Editorial Assistance: Emma Haines
Design/Typography: Stephen Bere
Cover Design: Dale Tomlinson
Cartography: Stephen Bere
Walk locations map: John Plumer
(JP Map Graphics Ltd)
Ordnance Survey mapping: The
National Map Centre, St Albans
Acting Head of Marketing: Tony Jerome

Photographs: Bob Steel
Additional photography: Cumbria Tourism/Ben Barden p53, p102;
Cumbria Tourism/Brian Sherwen p128; Cumbria Tourism/Dave Willis
p37, p63; Cumbria Tourism/Tony West p2-3, p38; Jim Chapple, p110

Cover photography: Top: Cumbria Tourism/Tony West; Left: Jon
Arnold Images Ltd/Alamy, Right: Ashley Cooper/Alamy
Back cover: Top: Cumbria Tourism/David Willis; Middle: Simon Cox;
Bottom: Cumbria Tourism/Tony West

As with any guide of this kind, being able to tap into local
knowledge and expertise is invaluable. Local CAMRA branches in
Furness; West Cumbria & Western Lakes; and Westmorland regularly visit pubs and keep abreast of quality issues. In particular I'd
like to thank David Stubbins and Jim Chapple for reviewing routes;
Chris Holland for input on Westmorland pubs; and David Currington
for sharing his detailed knowledge of the Kendal area.
Bob Steel

Contents

How to use this guide

The walks in this guide have been grouped into regions of the Lake District, all of which make suitable bases for forays into and around the national park. The walks are designed as day trips for visitors to the Lakes, or you could combine several of the routes for a longer walking holiday.

Overview map

This map can be found on page 12. It shows the locations of all the walks and is useful when planning a longer trip that takes in several of the walks, or organising transport and accommodation. Accommodation and transport information can be found on pages 153-154.

Walk information

Located on first page of each walk, this tinted box will give you some general information needed to plan your route including the start point, public transport access, distance, recommended Ordnance Survey map, and pubs visited. Further information about the walk such as terrain and suggested start time can often be found in the opening paragraph.

KEY FOR WALK MAPS

🏃	Walk start point
▬ ▬	Walk route
••••	Detour/Alternative route
🚩	Featured pub
🚩	'Try also' pub
A	Corresponds to grid reference in the text
➤	Direction of walk
🔍	Ordnance Survey grid reference
ℹ	Tourist Information Centre

Mapping

The routes are plotted on Ordnance Survey maps, with suggested detours clearly marked. The start (🏃), waypoints (A) and featured pubs (🚩) are marked on the map as shown. One grid square on the map equates to 1km square or 3/5 mile.

The routes

Featured pubs are numbered as they appear in the route and written in red. Other recommended pubs are numbered and written in blue. All other pubs are written in italics. Ordnance Survey grid references are marked with a (🔍) symbol, and those grid references shown on the map labelled with the corresponding letter (waypoints).

Information boxes

Tinted boxes give you information about local history, geography and other features of note.

Pub information

A blue box at the end of each walk gives you information about the pubs featured in the route, with information such as the opening hours and contact details – it is recommended that you phone ahead to check times with the pubs, as these can be subject to change. The numbered icons correspond with those in the text and on the map. This box also includes information about 'try also' pubs.

Introduction

Welcome to CAMRA's Lake District Pub Walks. England's largest national park is home to some of the country's most stunning scenery, and happily, also a wide variety of welcoming pubs serving an increasingly diverse range of beers from some of the best local breweries in the land. Most of the region is within the county of Cumbria, although the southern fringes belong to Lancashire.

The walks

The geography of Lakeland is rather like a large central dome with several valleys radiating out from close to the centre. Once these were filled with glaciers which later melted, and now lakes occupy many of the over-deepened valleys. The topography means that east–west and north–south travel across the Lake District can involve lengthy journeys, so the walks have been grouped together in such a way that the visitor who has a few days' holiday can attempt several routes without going too far. There are suggestions for links between routes, as in partner guides.

I hope that this book will encourage walkers to explore not only the most popular areas but also some of the less-frequented outlying areas of Lakeland where even a regular visitor may find previously undiscovered treasures – as I did when researching this book.

Most of the walks are rural and of 5–10 miles in length, but we have included three town walks too: in Ulverston, Kendal and Cockermouth.

The terrain and walk difficulty

The Lake District is home to England's highest mountains, but this doesn't mean to say that these are mountain walks. In fact many of them keep to the valleys where the scenery is often lush and green, and the terrain relatively straightforward. Nonetheless you will need a fair

**Wainwrights Inn,
Great Langdale**

level of fitness to enjoy the walks. Having mixed my walking and drinking for a good few years, I believe the best place for a good pub on a walk is, all else being equal, at or towards the end – the prospect of several stiff miles to cover after leaving the pub ought to temper mid-walk drinking. Accordingly, whilst many of the walks here have a mid-route stop, all of them offer a tempting pub at the finish of the day.

We have avoided simplistic numerical grading systems for walk difficulty in favour of descriptive assessments of the degree of challenge including the navigational difficulties. Most routes are easy to follow as signage is generally good – as befits a national park with a well-maintained network of paths. It's always a good idea to carry a reliable map in addition to using the maps in this guide, and on some routes where there are stretches across open country, confidence in reading the map and the landscape will also help, as will basic compass skills. That said, with the exception of a few higher-level routes which carry clear warnings, most of the routes in the book can be enjoyed by the leisure walker.

The pubs

CAMRA's passionate interest is cask ale, and the quality of it. Local branches of the Campaign monitor Cumbria's pubs regularly and all the pubs in this guide are here on the approval of those branches. CAMRA also encourages pubs to offer a warm welcome, serve good food and maintain the convivial atmosphere which makes the British pub a unique institution. I'm a great believer in the adage that pubs are not restaurants, and that they should always welcome the casual drinker who is not dining. Nor should they, as a few still do, extend a frosty greeting to walkers who have muddy boots! I can think of 'pubs' at over 1,000 feet high in moorland areas where the whole place is heavily carpeted and with a décor more suited to central London than the mountains. Having said this, unlike other pub walks books most of the routes in this guide pass more than one pub; this way you can choose how many to visit, and use the descriptions to go for the one(s) which suit(s) you.

Public transport

Public transport is variable in availability across Lakeland, and generally buses are not as plentiful as in the Peak District, location of a partner guide to this book. The railhead at Windermere, which now has direct services from the large towns of the North West, is a key entry point to the area, but the very useful coastal rail route via Ulverston and Ravenglass is also an invaluable asset to the user of this guide – a disproportionate number of the walks are found close to the southern and western fringes of the region, served by this line, and Furness in particular is a treasury

of wonderful walks served by a portfolio of top-quality pubs.

Bus routes run from the larger towns and serve the majority of the routes in this book, but many of these services are seasonal, and the winter visitor will have to make alternative arrangements on many routes. A widely-available timetable of the main bus routes is a very useful resource, and tourist offices will advise on local services. On the internet, consult www.traveline. org.uk

Facilities for the disabled and children; and animals

We have not included information on access for disabled visitors, as this changes all the time, and it's best to ring ahead and check.

Many pubs welcome children, especially before 9pm, either in the whole pub or in a designated area. Of course if you're walking with young people once again you may be well advised to ask ahead, especially if there are no alternative venues on the route.

Similarly dog owners will know that pub policy towards their pets varies considerably so once again the advice is, check ahead. Contact details for every pub can be found on the walk pages.

Enjoy the walks!
Bob Steel

**Early morning
landscape, Appleby**

Walking safety

The countryside code

When walking in the Lake District, or anywhere else in the countryside, it's always worth following a few simple, common-sense guidelines.

Walking poles can be useful aids

• Plan ahead and be prepared for the unexpected. Bad weather and restricted access to land – for example, during breeding season or crop spraying – may force you to alter you plans, so follow local signs and advice and don't be afraid to turn back.

• Leave gates as you find them. The countryside is a working area and even well-intentioned actions can affect people's livelihoods and the welfare of animals.

• Protect the appearance, flora and fauna of the Lake District by taking your litter home.

• If you're walking with a dog, keep it under control. It's your responsibility to make sure your dog is not a nuisance or a danger to farm animals, wildlife or other people.

• Consider other people – other walkers, riders and cyclists and those who work and live in the countryside.

What to wear and what to take

Many readers will be experienced walkers and may not need any advice, but if you're relatively new to walking the following tips may be useful.

• Make sure you are well-equipped, for comfort as well as safety.

• Trainers or walking shoes with good grip are fine, but walking boots are recommended for more demanding terrain. They provide support for your ankles, which is useful when tackling steep slopes, and keep your feet warm and dry. A thick pair of socks will make them more comfortable in cold weather too.

• Always pack enough clothing to wear for any potential turn in the weather. It's a good idea to have layers of clothes so that you can take one off or put one on as you warm up or the weather cools down. A waterproof jacket will keep off both rain and wind, with hoods and pockets being particularly useful features. Fleeces are good to wear in between your 'base layer' and jacket, especially ones with zips as they allow you to cool off easily if necessary. Avoid jeans – they take a long time to dry if they get wet. Light-weight, loose-fitting trousers made from synthetic material are favoured by walkers. They dry quickly and have handy pockets for carrying maps. Waterproof over-trousers or gaiters will prevent trousers and socks from getting wet.

• Wear sun hats and sun cream in summer, if need be, and take plenty of water to drink. It's a good idea to carry something to eat – even if it's only a couple of cereal bars.

• A rucksack can be very useful – use it to carry any spare clothing and food as well as other essentials like a map, compass, mobile phone, emergency whistle, torch, and simple first aid kit.

• The maps and directions in this book will help you follow the walks, but if you want to venture off the beaten track to do a little more exploring on your own, or even connect sections of different walks from the book, a map and compass are invaluable – provided you know how to use them. Each walk lists the relevant Ordnance Survey map in its introduction, as well as grid reference points along the route.

Saftey on the roads

Some of the routes include short stretches on rural lanes and roads. In general these are not very busy, but always take care as sometimes vehicles appear suddenly and travel quickly (especially on country roads with national speed limits). If there is not a footpath, walk in single file on the right-hand side (facing the traffic) except on corners and bends with poor visibility when you should cross (carefully) to get a better view.

Public transport

If relying on public transport, it is always worth checking the time of the last train or bus back to where you are staying before setting out on your day's walk, and noting down the number of a local taxi firm should you get into difficulties.

The award-winning Jennings Brewery

The Cumbrian brewing scene; an ongoing success story

In recent years Cumbria has seen huge growth in the number of beers on offer and breweries brewing them. It wasn't long ago that a visitor to Lakeland's pubs had little more than Hobson's choice when it came to real ale: in most pubs it was either Hartleys of Ulverston or Jennings of Cockermouth. Things started to change In the mid 1980s when Hartleys were acquired by Robinson's of Stockport, but perhaps more significantly in 1986 – the year Matthew Brown closed the Lion Brewery in Workington – when Peter Yates, an ex Jennings head brewer, started commercial brewing at his microbrewery in Westnewton. This was to be the first 'micro' in Cumbria, followed two years later by the Hesket Newmarket brewery at the rear of the Old Crown pub in the village. The Old Crown is also notable as the country's first successful community-owned pub, and is now a lively and successful local.

There has been a steady trickle of new breweries ever since, but equally important for the visiting drinker is the quality of the beers they produce, evidenced by a string of awards, and steady growth in many of them. For example, just three years after brewing at Coniston started in 1998, Coniston Bluebird won the Champion Beer of Britain accolade at the Great British Beer Festival. Nearby, the Hawkshead brewery has been so successful that they have recently moved to far bigger premises in Staveley. Not even the acrimonious closure by Robinson's of the Hartleys Brewery in Ulverston in 1991 has been able to blunt the steady and growing confidence in the Cumbrian brewing scene: several pubs brew their own beer, some, notably the Loweswater brewery at the award-winning Kirkstile Inn outgrowing their nest and moving out to larger premises. Perhaps it is this confident and competitive brewing scene along with a lively campaign from CAMRA which helped persuade new owners Wolverhampton & Dudley (later to become Marston's) to keep Jennings' Castle Brewery open, and not to use the disastrous 2009 floods in Cockermouth as an excuse to close it. The good news is that they invested and continue to invest heavily in the site and the brewery re-opened early in 2010.

As we stand, Cumbria currently has 29 operational breweries, large and small; a remarkable number for a county with less than 500,000 residents. At a conservative estimate there are over 100 Cumbrian-brewed 'regular' beers available around the county at any one time, with the addition of a similar number of seasonals and one-offs, and you'll find plenty of evidence for the healthy state of the Lake District brewing economy on many of the walks in this book.

The other initiative which Cumbrian pubs have seized upon enthusiastically is CAMRA's LocAle scheme. This aims to promote locally-brewed beers, and in an area where geography makes inward deliveries lengthy, pubs have seized upon the opportunity of serving local ales with gusto.

Check www.cumbriacamra.org.uk for updates on pubs, breweries and the real-ale scene in Cumbria.

With thanks to Jim Chapple and David Stubbins

Beer styles

You can deepen your appreciation of cask ale with this run-down on the main styles available.

Bitter

Towards the end of the 19th century, brewers moved away from vatted beers stored for many months and developed 'running beers' that could be served after a few days' storage in pub cellars. Bitter was generally deep bronze to copper in colour due to the use of darker malts that give the beer fullness of palate. Best is a stronger version of Bitter but there is considerable crossover. Bitter falls into the 3.4% to 3.9% band, with Best Bitter 4% upwards, but a number of brewers label their ordinary Bitters 'Best'. A further development of Bitter comes in the shape of Extra or Special Strong Bitters of 5% or more. With ordinary Bitter, look for a spicy, peppery and grassy hop character, a powerful bitterness, tangy fruit and juicy and nutty malt. With Best and Strong Bitters, malt and fruit character will tend to dominate.

Golden Ales

This new style of pale, well-hopped and quench-ing beer developed in the 1980s as independent brewers attempted to win younger drinkers from heavily-promoted lager brands. Strengths will range from 3.5% to 5%. The hallmark will be the biscuity and juicy malt character derived from pale malts, underscored by tart citrus fruit and peppery hops, often with the addition of hints of vanilla and sweetcorn. Above all, such beers are quenching and served cool.

IPA and Pale Ale

India Pale Ale changed the face of brewing early in the 19th century. The new technologies of the Industrial Revolution enabled brewers to use pale malts to fashion beers that were genuinely golden or pale bronze in colour. First brewed in London and Burton-on-Trent for the colonial market, IPAs were strong in alcohol and high in hops: the preservative character of the hops helped keep the beers in good condition during long sea journeys. Beers with less alcohol and hops were developed for the domestic market and were known as Pale Ale. Look for juicy malt, citrus fruit and a big spicy, peppery, bitter hop character, with strengths of 4% upwards.

Mild

Mild was once the most popular style of beer, but was overtaken in popularity by Bitter from the 1950s. It was developed in the 18th and 19th centuries as a less aggressively bitter style of beer than porter and stout. Early Milds were much stronger that modern interpretations, which tend to fall in the 3% to 3.5% category. Look for rich malty aromas and flavours with hints of dark fruit, chocolate, coffee and caramel and a gentle underpinning of hop bitterness.

Old Ale

Old ale recalls the type of beer brewed before the Industrial Revolution, stored for months or even years in unlined wooden vessels known as tuns. The beer would pick up some lactic sourness as a result of wild yeasts, lactobacilli and tannins in the wood. The result was a beer dubbed 'stale' by drinkers: it was one of the components of the early, blended Porters. Old ales, contrary to expectation, do not have to be especially strong: they can be no more than 4% alcohol. Neither do they have to be dark: old ale can be pale and burst with lush sappy malt, tart fruit and spicy hop notes.

Porter and Stout

Porter was a London style that turned the brewing industry upside down early in the 18th century. It was a dark brown beer that was originally a blend of brown ale, pale ale and old ale. It acquired its name as a result of its popularity among London's market porters. The strongest versions of Porter were known as Stout Porter, or simply Stout. Such vast quantities of Porter and Stout flooded into Ireland from London and Bristol that a Dublin brewer named Arthur Guinness decided to fashion his own interpretation of the style. Guinness in Dublin blended some unmalted roasted barley and in so doing produced a style known as Dry Irish Stout. Look for profound dark and roasted malt character with raisin and sultana fruit, espresso or cappuccino coffee, liquorice and molasses.

With thanks to Roger Protz

Lake District overview map

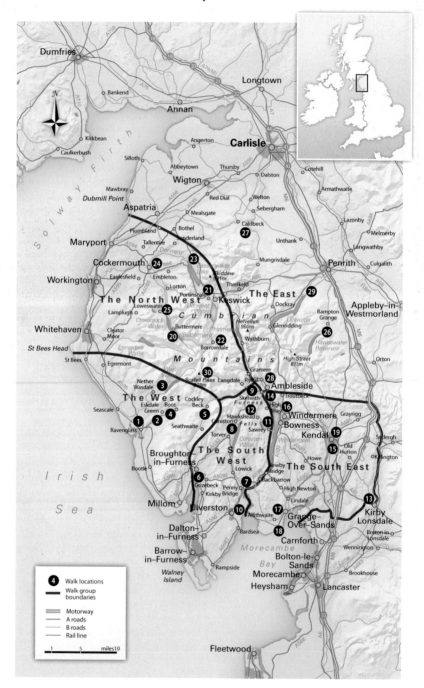

Copeland Group –
the West

Descent into Boot

National park meets the sea: Ravenglass

WALK INFORMATION

Start/Finish: Ravenglass stations

Access: Trains from Barrow-in-Furness/Foxfield

Distance: 3.7 miles (5.9km)

OS map: OS Explorer OL6

Key attractions: Roman bath house; Ravenglass & Eskdale Railway; Muncaster Castle & gardens

The pubs: Ratty Arms, Holly House, both Ravenglass. Try also: Brown Cow, Waberthwaite

Occupying an enviable position on the estuaries of the little Esk and Irt Rivers, Ravenglass is little more than a village street fronting the sea – but with its peaceful setting and attractive cottages the town manages to endear itself to the great majority of its visitors. Moreover it has a long history going back to Roman times, with one of the best-preserved Roman buildings in the country a stone's throw from our route. Both the walking and the navigation are at a pretty easy level and the whole walk can be done comfortably in a couple of hours.

Ravenglass is on the useful Cumbria Coast Railway and at the terminus of the Ravenglass and Eskdale Railway, or La'al Ratty as it's affectionately known. Nearby are the renowned gardens of Muncaster Castle, which date back to the 18th century and are home to one of Europe's largest collections of rhododendrons. The walk itself takes in some interesting coastal and river habitats as well as some pleasant wooded stretches where, in season, more rhododendrons will add plenty of colour. For a small place there's a very good beer range on offer in the two featured pubs and those with their own transport or access to a cab might well extend this by visiting the Brown Cow at nearby Waberthwaite.

The foreshore at Ravenglass, opposite the Holly House

The well-preserved Roman bath house

Key

- **– – – –** Walk route
- **· · · · · ·** Alternative route

The walk starts at the mainline station which stands right next to both the Ratty Arms and the terminus of the Ravenglass & Eskdale Railway. Before setting off you might wish to visit the café on the latter which opens early and offers a range of tempting treats to get the day off to a good start. From the station car park walk down to the village main street which fronts the shore.

Ravenglass has a fascinating history: the only coastal village in the Lake District national park, it was an important base for the Romans, who called it Glannoventa and occupied it with a garrison of 1,000 soldiers for around 300 years.

On the Ravenglass Estuary looking towards Black Combe

Ravenglass was granted a charter by King John in 1208, and was a busy port taking in goods brought across the Irish Sea until the 1800s when the harbour began to silt up. Smugglers did well for a while, but today it's a sleepy place in comparison.

A charming collection of cottages line the open aspect to the sea; you'll pass Holly House which we will return to later, but walk to the left past the Post Office stores and *Pennington* hotel down to the end of the road which leads straight onto the beach. The Bay Horse on your left, now a guest house, was one of several pubs when the town was more important than it is now.

At all but the highest tides it's an easy matter to bear left along the foreshore and, on reaching the end of the little bay with some Ministry of Defence land ahead, the bridleway bears right onto a grassy terrace with very good views out across the estuary and the dunes, before dropping you down some steps to the shore once again, and following the shore southwards. At low tide you'll get a salty tang in your nostrils. Ignore the path bearing left under the railway as this is a dead end as far as our walk is concerned; behind you the towers of the Sellafield processing plant are now visible. Progress is easier a little beyond here if you follow the wall as its bears inland just a little rather than keeping to the muddy foreshore. As you'd expect, birdlife is profuse on this estuary and if you're a bird watcher you'll be busy with your binoculars along this stretch; inland the larger fells of Lakeland are visible.

Soon the Eskmeals railway viaduct comes into view beyond which the rounded slopes of Black Combe (1,967 feet) are visible. This outlying fell is so isolated from others that the view from the summit is said to be one of the most extensive in the country. This is where the route leaves the estuary and swings inland to cross under the railway line. The scenery changes fairly abruptly as you find yourself walking on a very good path between an attractive wooded escarpment and the tall reeds and grasses fringing the River Esk's floodplain. Look for a prominent gate just to the left where the path runs down towards the shore to the Ordnance Survey's ridiculous 'ford' marked on the map, which seems to be little more than a contribution to stabilising the population!

Once through the gate (with a Cumbria Coastal Way sign inside) you are in shady woodland. In 20 yards bear left (the path right is a concessionary route skirting Muncaster Castle) and then almost immediately (50 yards) right (with 'Alternative Route' sign) through a kissing gate and now onto a grassy fellside aiming for the gate in the wall straight ahead. Go through this and turn left onto a wider track with the wall on your left. If the weather is fine you'll get a wonderful view of the Isle of Man through breaks in this wall. On your right the land rises up to Newtown Knott.

Reach the house at Newtown ignoring the first path on the right to Muncaster Castle but bearing right onto the next wide path a few yards beyond the exit driveway from the house on your left, (A, 093957) unless you want to cut proceedings short at this point in which case continue ahead on the track which leads back down to the village past the Roman bath house (see below). Our route takes you gently but steadily uphill with trees on both sides, and the only thing likely to

THE RAVENGLASS & ESKDALE RAILWAY

'Ratty' was opened in 1875 as an industrial line at 3-foot gauge to carry iron ore from workings near Boot to the coast at Ravenglass. However, the ore was limited in quantity and the mines never really made any money, even with ore prices of 30/- a ton following the hike in steel prices caused by the Franco-Prussian war. By the time the railway was completed to Boot in 1875, ore prices were falling and the numerous levels driven down the hillside had shown just how little ore was present. The line limped on for a considerable time after this, carrying a little granite from a mine near Beckfoot and a small amount of agricultural and tourist traffic, but was finally closed in 1913. The narrow gauge (15 inch or 381mm) railway we see today was re-laid during the Great War by two Narrow Gauge enthusiasts, carrying passengers from the start but also goods traffic from a quarry near Beckfoot. By 1946 ownership had transferred to the Keswick Granite Company, who decided in 1953 to cease quarrying operations. It looked like the end of the line in 1960 when closure was announced but the Ravenglass & Eskdale Railway Preservation Society was formed by enthusiasts and a couple of buyers were found to stump up the monies at the auction of stock. Since then the line has gone from strength to strength with the busiest timetable of any preserved line in the region and several new locomotives, mostly steam. In 2007 a new station and visitor centre at the Dalegarth terminus was opened.

'Ratty' station at Ravenglass

Drinkers outside the Holly House

disturb you here is the bird song. Reach a good sized mature pond, beyond which the landscape becomes more open. Just before you reach the octagonal entrance hut to Muncaster Castle and gardens, which of course you may wish to detour and visit now or later, head left on an unsigned path which passes some farm buildings before emerging on the relatively busy main road at Muncaster Home Farm. Cross this carefully to the pavement opposite and continue in more or less the same direction down the hill for a few hundred yards until you reach a sharp right-hand bend; then, choosing your spot carefully so that you can see in both directions, cross the road again and take the marked path which leaves the road at this point on the left.

This is a very appealing stretch of old woodland which in turn feeds out via a kissing gate onto an open area with great views over the estuary. The right of way passes midway under the two pylons ahead down towards a second gate whereupon it bears 90-degrees right and exits the farmland via a third gate giving onto a stony track.

At this point, unless you visited earlier, I recommend you turn left and walk back up the track for five minutes to visit the Roman bath house. Little still remains of the large Roman fort except for the remarkable bath house, also known as Walls Castle. This is one of the largest surviving Roman structures in England, about 40ft x 90ft with walls over 12 foot high (the highest remaining Roman walls in Britain).

Back at the path junction, the path ahead under the railway line brings you back down to the

bay at the end of the main street, but the quickest way back to Ravenglass station is to bear right on the wide track for about 300 yards and then left through into a small paddock with the footbridge by the station at the far end.

It's very plain from this angle that the **Ratty Arms** occupies the old station building on the mainline. To get in walk around it to the rear. It's a good conversion which has resulted in a pubby character, with a veranda extension which looks out onto the platforms. As will become quite a theme in the walks in this book the Ratty has taken the advantage of the renaissance of real ale in Cumbria and offers a good range of beers: two guests (usually Cumbrian) complement the Jennings Cumberland, Theakston Black Bull and Greene King Ruddles County. There's a decent food menu until about 8 o'clock. When you're done, it's just a short walk down to the main street where you'll find the **Holly House** facing the sea. Tacked onto the side of a hotel it also offers a surprisingly pub-like atmosphere with two distinct areas within the small flagstoned public bar. Better still, there are up to five well-kept beers, with Jennings, Moorhouses and Cumbrian micros prominent. Food is available as you'd expect from a hotel operation.

If you're still game for another pub you could try the *Pennington* down the street, which usually has a couple of Cumbrian micros on, or if you have your own transport, a couple of miles south down the A595 road (NOT over the ford!!) the well regarded **Brown Cow** in Waberthwaite (off map) has up to seven cask ales on tap.

PUB INFORMATION

1 Ratty Arms
Ravenglass, CA18 1SN
01229 717676
rattyarms@aol.com
Opening Hours: 11 (12 Sun) -11

2 Holly House
Main Street, Ravenglass,
CA18 1SQ
01229 717230
rachelfrangy@yahoo.co.uk
Opening Hours: 11-11; 12-10.30 Sun

TRY ALSO:

Brown Cow
Waberthwaite, Millom, LA19 5YJ
01229 717243
www.thebrowncowinn.com
Opening Hours: 11.30-11;
12-10.30 Sun

Over Muncaster Fell to Eskdale

WALK INFORMATION

Start: Muncaster Mill station, Ravenglass & Eskdale Railway (⊙ 095977)

Finish: Irton Road station, Ravenglass & Eskdale Railway

Access: Trains (La'al Ratty) to Muncaster Mill station

Distance: To Bower House Inn and return to Irton Road station, 5.3 miles (8.6km)

OS map: OS Explorer OL6

Key attractions: Roman bath house; Ravenglass & Eskdale Railway; Muncaster Castle & gardens; Sellafield visitor centre (9 miles)

The pubs: Bower House Inn, Eskdale. Try also: George IV, Eskdale

Harter Fell and Eskdale from Muncaster Fell

Muncaster Fell — a long, relatively low-lying ridge covered with bracken, gorse and other vegetation — is crossed by an excellent path which lets you enjoy the fine views without much toil. Doing the walk in the recommended direction enables you to make the best of the scenery: you can see out to the coast and beyond behind you, whilst ahead lie the big hills surrounding the green valley of Eskdale, which Ruskin called "the gateway to Paradise". Making good use of the 'Ratty' railway will enable you to enjoy the pubs in the quiet valleys at the far end before returning to Ravenglass which is an obvious base for this walk. Thanks to the good path across the fell, navigation is on the whole pretty straightforward, and apart from a stiff pull at the start, gradients are mild. There may be some wet stretches but nothing to cause serious problems for well-shod walkers.

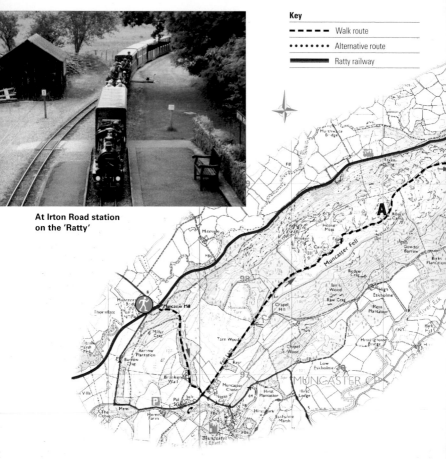

Key

- – – – – Walk route
- • • • • • • Alternative route
- ▬▬▬▬▬ Ratty railway

At Irton Road station on the 'Ratty'

The walk starts at the Muncaster Mill station on the La'al Ratty: if you arrive by train remember it's a request stop so tell the guard as you're getting on! Pick up the path almost opposite the station exit gate, marked by white posts, which climbs up through the vegetation to meet and cross a wider bridleway: our route is signed 'Castle'. There's also a car park by the station with space for several vehicles, in which case take the bridleway directly from the car park until it meets the path from the station (at which point you'll bear right).

This first section beyond here is the steepest of the whole walk so take your time as you climb up and eventually level out, ignoring paths meeting from right to left, until in about 20 minutes you reach a gate in sight of the main road

beyond. Turn left on the good path here to reach the main road in another five minutes or so. You're very close to the entrance to Muncaster gardens here if you plan to visit *en route*.

At this point bear left onto Fell Lane. Climb steadily, and at a clear fork in the paths bear right, but beyond this where the bridleway turns off right at 90-degrees, continue ahead on the footpath marked 'Eskdale'. Almost immediately on your left here is the rather attractive Muncaster Tarn which might be a good spot for a rest and your flask if you have one

Muncaster Fell is one of several relatively low-lying hills around the central Lake District which Wainwright included in his book of so-called outlying fells, suggesting in the typically non-PC terms of his day that these would be suitable

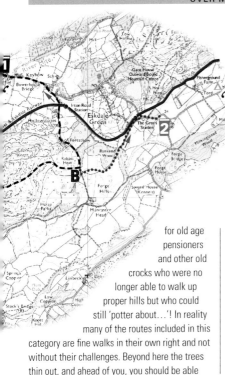

for old age pensioners and other old crocks who were no longer able to walk up proper hills but who could still 'potter about…'! In reality many of the routes included in this category are fine walks in their own right and not without their challenges. Beyond here the trees thin out, and ahead of you, you should be able to catch sight of the trig point which marks the summit of this long and narrow fell. Across to your left a wide vista across the Cumbrian coastal plain begins to open out, with the Sellafield re-processing plant rather too conspicuous for comfort. Beyond Sellafield the prominent headland is St Bee's Head, the start of the Coast to Coast walk. Climb up to the trig point from where, because there are no other intervening fells nearby, the view is very extensive despite the relatively modest height of just over 750 feet.

Descending towards Eskdale Green after the walk across Muncaster Fell

From left to right you may be able to pick out Red Pike, Yewbarrow, Illgill Head, the Scafells and Harter Fell which is very prominent to the right, and then the Coniston group. Behind you of course, the Irish Sea and – conditions permitting – the Isle of Man should be visible.

Leaving the summit, descend steeply down and rejoin the very good path which will take you comfortably through the heavily vegetated undulating summit ridge which would, without a path, be absolute purgatory to progress through. The springy, peaty turf makes going underfoot very easy. Beyond the point marked 'Ross's Camp' on the map (A, ⊙ 121987) the route crosses a rather boggy area before heading downhill to a wall ahead; pass through the gateway at the left-hand end of this wall so that you are now walking, for about five minutes, with a wall immediately on your left before the path starts snaking away to the right a little making for a gap between a larger and a smaller rocky knoll ahead of you.

The path continues to be very straightforward with pleasant views ahead into the wooded valley of Eskdale – filling the view it's still Harter Fell which catches the eye with its shapely peak. After a few more minutes you should arrive at the gate in the corner of a wall, which you pass through and continue down (ignore the grassy path doubling back uphill to the left before the gate). Reach the bridleway (B, ⊙ 139993), and at this point turn left – although you may wish to try your luck at the **George IV 2** first (see

box) by going on through the gate on the right and then bearing left almost immediately on the pathway which will take you down into Eskdale Green whereupon the pub is a short walk to the right (see map). Otherwise, continue along this good bridleway ignoring the path to the right, past Forest Howe, where it becomes a tarmac road which crosses the 'Ratty' right by Irton Road station. If you haven't done so already, check the train times, since you may well want these on the way home. Then simply walk down to the road junction in front of you and bear left, whereupon it's about six or seven minutes to walk down what is usually a fairly quiet road – although there is no footpath – to reach the **Bower House Inn 1**. From the outside, this 17th-century coaching inn oozes the sort of character that comes from a good age, and in that context the comfortable and carpeted interior of this hotel feels a bit over-modernised to lovers of traditional buildings. That said, there's still some appeal left, notably in a small corner near the bar with its own fireplace and several old beams. The emphasis is on the local with both food and drink: expect at least three changing beers, often from Yates or Keswick, with the tasty house beer brewed by the competent Ennerdale brewery. The place takes its food very seriously and you can eat well here at reasonable prices.

There's plenty of opportunity here if you want to go *off piste* with your map, or if you're done then just retrace your steps to return down the lane to Irton Road station to fetch your train.

PUB INFORMATION

1 **Bower House Inn**
Eskdale Green, CA19 1TD
01946 723244
www.bowerhouseinn.co.uk
Opening Hours: 11-11; 12-10.30 Sun

TRY ALSO:

2 **George IV**
Eskdale Green, CA19 1TS
01946 723262
www.kinggeorge-eskdale.co.uk
Opening Hours: 11-11

Wastwater & Netherwasdale

WALK INFORMATION

Start/Finish: Strands village (Nether Wasdale). An alternative start is the lake shore road (some limited parking), allowing you to finish at the Wasdale Hall youth hostel

Access: Limited public transport: demand responsive taxi bus operated by Gosforth taxis from Seascale via Gosforth, tel 01946 725308

Distance: 5 miles (8km)

OS map: OS Explorer OL6

Key attractions: Wastwater and Screes; Ravenglass & Eskdale Railway (2 miles); Gosforth pottery (5 miles); Sellafield visitor centre (9 miles)

The pubs: Strands Hotel, Screes, both Strands. Try also: Wasdale Hall, Wasdale

Wasdale Valley is the remotest and one of the most tranquil corners of the Lake District. Wastwater itself – owned by the National Trust – is a glacial lake half a mile wide, three miles in length and is England's deepest at 258 feet. England's most magnificent mountains including its highest, Scafell Pike, form a horseshoe backdrop. Wordsworth described Wastwater as "long, narrow, stern and desolate", and in 2007, a TV poll concluded that the views along the lake here were Britain's best, which I wouldn't disagree with. This walk traverses some little-used paths on the northern side of the lake under the slopes of rugged Buckbarrow, before returning to the picture-postcard village green at Strands. Despite the lofty hills all around, the walk is not at all demanding and the five miles go by pretty easily.

The route follows the shore path along Wastwater

Key

- - - - - Walk route

Think about timings on this walk: consider starting on a summer afternoon to arrive at Wasdale Hall after opening at 5pm and returning to Strands in time for an evening meal.

From the centre of the village of Strands (also known as Nether Wasdale), where the two pubs which we'll be visiting later face each other across the lawns, head out east on the road. You almost immediately pass the little gas-lit St Michael's church on the left. Originally a chapel of ease for the splendid 12th-century St Bees priory, this 16th-century church is worth a visit for its oak panelling, pulpit and lectern which were all salvaged following a fire at York Minster after a fire in the 19th century. The ceiling has some fine plaster reliefs.

Cross the little Cinderdale Bridge and bear right (signed 'Santon Bridge'), crossing Forest Bridge just beyond the next road junction. Here look for a left turn down a signed route along a farm track (signed 'Wasdale') which leads to Esthwaite Farm.

Wasdale Hall youth hostel offers real ale on handpump to non-residents

On this track you'll get your first glimpse of the horseshoe of big fells, including Great Gable, which encircle the head of Wastwater. Follow through the farm buildings and swing left down the farm track rather than taking the footpath over the stile. Straight ahead is a knoll covered by native woodland, which you will shortly be entering; and when the lane curves around to the

Shared path near Strands

right you'll see a footpath sign pointing straight ahead by a gate with a wall running off to the left. Through the gate, keeping the wall and later the hedge on your left, follow this path down towards Lund Bridge over the River Irt, which you will see when you reach the foot of the slope. This is the same river we encountered in walks 1 and 2, which has its source in the glacial lake. Don't worry if you overshoot – you'll simply reach the river and be forced back to your left to reach the bridge. Once across here and through the kissing gate, you're into a wooded knoll at the southern end of the lake. Take the permitted path around to the right which leads you pleasantly back towards the River Irt. The path now follows the widening stream as it opens out into the lake,

and as the water widens the wonderful view up Wastwater opens up. It's difficult to argue with the contention that this is the finest view in England except possibly the reverse view from the top of Great Gable down towards the lake. If the weather is favourable it's a good spot to rest and admire the view. The lake is England's deepest, at 258 feet, despite the surface being 200 feet above sea level.

A little further along you pass the lakeside **Wasdale Hall** 3, now a youth hostel and one which opens to non-residents for the sale of, among other things, local real ale usually in the form of a beer from Hesket Newmarket.

Continue along the lakeshore path until eventually, passing through some rhododendrons, the track climbs via a ladder stile to meet the narrow unfenced road which runs along the western shore of the lake. Continue walking along the verge with good views all around. If you haven't seen them before the impressive screes of Wastwater across the lake in particular will catch your attention. They are without doubt the best-known screes in the country and are mightily impressive.

About a quarter of a mile along the road there's a junction, and also some parking if you wish to start the route from here. Double back on the even quieter unfenced lane running west and rising gently under the steep slopes of Buckbarrow, for the best part of a mile. Would that all road walking was as pleasant as this!

Just short of some farm buildings on your left a bridleway sign directs you down (signed

The two pubs overlook the lovely village green at Strands

LEFT: **Strands Hotel**   RIGHT: **Screes**

'Cinderdale Bridge 1¼ miles'). Take this bridleway down to the farm and through onto a walled lane for a couple of hundred yards; it then swings around to the left and then right. At the point in a further 200 yards or so where the bridleway turns sharply left at a gate, a stile (with a signpost marked 'footpath Strands') continuing the path straight ahead is the route we wish to take. Continue in the same direction crossing another bridleway where, despite the broken fingerpost, the path to Strands continues straight ahead onto the open grassy fell.

Go through the wall just to the left of three oak trees where you should find a stone step stile, to merge with another footpath coming in from the right along a second wall. Although the wall now veers off to the left the trajectory of the path continues straight ahead – a big wide grassy avenue points the way with a clump of conifer trees over to your right and soon a ladder stile ahead of you takes you into a more overgrown area with some wet areas crossed by wooden walkboards before another ladder stile. You've now reached the brow of the hill – the view ahead is of a small camp site and the buildings of Strands. The path drops down and skirts the edge of the camp site before reaching the road where you turn right and you'll need no more help to find the two pubs on opposite sides of the village

green where we started. Not to be missed is the **Strands Hotel** 1 with its microbrewery. Smartly refurbished with an appealing wooden bar top, the main bar room is complemented by a smaller lower room down some stairs. CAMRA awards line the walls. Two guest beers, usually from Jennings, join the hotel's own beers including the quirkily named T'err-minator stout. In an area where much of the income derives from food (and there's a wide menu here) it's perhaps difficult to complain too loudly about the practice of reserving so many of the tables for diners; but be aware that if you're 'only' drinking here at busy times you may be confined – not a problem in good weather of course as there is some attractive outside seating. It's the pub across the road, the **Screes** 2 which has the best deal of the village green, with tables outside the pub sitting on the lawn. The multi-roomed layout has survived, with a stone-flagged lower room retaining a good deal of character. The pub sign is worth looking out for. Where the Screes can't compete with their neighbour is in beer choice. Screes is tied to Robinson's who acquired this former Hartleys house.

If you have access to your own transport, Wasdale Head, a few miles further up the valley, is home to the famous climbers' hotel and real-ale venue the *Wasdale Head Inn* (see walk 30).

PUB INFORMATION

1 **Strands Hotel**
Strands, CA20 1ET
019467 26237
www.strandshotel.com
Opening Hours:
11-11; 12-10.30 Sun

2 **Screes**
Strands, CA20 1ET
019467 26262
www.thescrees.co.uk
Opening Hours: 11-11

TRY ALSO:

3 **Wasdale Hall**
Wasdale, CA20 1ET
01629 592700
www.yha.org.uk
Opening Hours: 5-11

Boot & Upper Eskdale

WALK INFORMATION

Start: Beckfoot station, Ravenglass & Eskdale Railway

Finish: Dalegarth station, Ravenglass & Eskdale Railway

Access: Trains (La'al Ratty) from Ravenglass

Distance: 4.5 miles (7.2km)

OS map: OS Explorer OL6

Key attractions: Hardknott Pass and Roman Fort; Eskdale Mill; Stanley Ghyll Force (waterfall)

The pubs: Boot Inn, Brook House Inn, both Boot; Woolpack Inn, Eskdale;

The river Esk can lay claim to being one of England's most mountainous streams, but here in its middle reaches it meanders in a wide, flat glacial valley through some of the prettiest woodland in Cumbria. The three pubs on this walk offer a fabulous range of well-kept beers, and although they play host between them to the Boot beer festival each June, in truth they constitute a permanent beer festival with more than enough choice to satisfy the most discriminating of imbibers! The walk, which makes use of the La'al Ratty railway for access, starts by taking you steeply up on the fellside to visit Blea Tarn before rewarding you with a visit to Boot's pubs, interspersed with a much less strenuous riverside section; although of course couch potatoes could cheat by sneaking along from the railhead to pub number one without tackling the hillside and without anyone finding out...

Descent into Boot

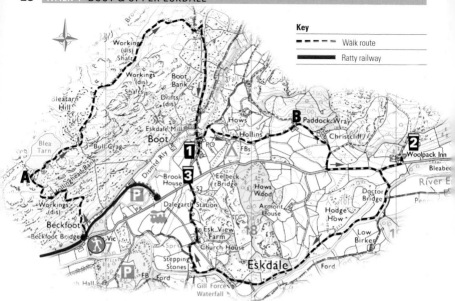

Start the walk at the Beckfoot halt on the 'Ratty', a short distance west of the terminus at Dalegarth. There's also a pull-in for a few cars alongside and another car parking space about 150 yards further along the road.

Set off by crossing the rail tracks on the simple level crossing and following the signed path which tackles the hillside directly. By pub walk standards this is a stiff climb and you'd be advised to take your time. As a partial reward, excellent views of the Eskdale Valley open up quickly and you'll see the small hamlet of Boot with its pubs about a mile away. When you reach a cairn near the brow of the climb (A, ⊙ 165007) bear right and walk up the final part to Blea Tarn which makes an obvious place to rest awhile as well as being a scenic spot especially if the sun is shining.

Setting off again, take the well-worn path along the right-hand side of the tarn which then climbs up steeply again through the col (pass) before levelling off at last with a rewarding panorama stretching from Red Pike on your left to Scafell ahead of you and round to Harter Fell and the Coniston hills on your right. Follow the cairns and at a fork in the path take the more distinct right-hand option which passes a small fenced-off mineshaft – probably part of the old Nab Gill workings – and starts descending, keeping a broken wall over on your right and dropping down

IRON ORE MINING IN ESKDALE

The low-grade iron ore Haematite occurs in small quantities in Eskdale, and has been smelted in the valley since at least Roman times. The first proper mines go back to early Victorian times and by 1841 seven mines are listed in the Eskdale census, with ore being exported from Ravenglass. Later in the century it was the iron ore trade which stimulated the construction of the 'Ratty' (see box, walk 1). Despite a surge in ore prices the mines were never really economic – numerous levels driven down the hillside had shown just how little ore was present. In total the valley produced perhaps 100,000 tons of iron ore over the centuries, approximately the tonnage the railway was built to carry in one year!

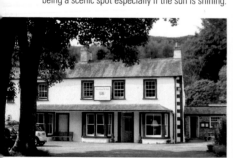

The Woolpack Inn, Upper Eskdale

through some ruined huts, again probably associated with the old mine (see box). Ahead of you is the Whillan Beck valley which leads down to Boot; and the pretty clear path will lead you around to the right and steadily downhill towards the hamlet. On your left as you enter the picturesque little settlement is the late-16th century Eskdale Mill, in a charming spot with the stream and waterwheels at the rear. It houses an exhibition explaining the whole milling process and the workings of the wooden machinery, which is still in working order. In its later life the mill was used to generate electricity – mains power didn't arrive in the valley until 1955.

The walk follows the Esk valley through woodland

A short distance further down on the right is the first of our three pub stops, the **Boot Inn** **1**, with its attractive garden. It has a spacious and comfortable interior offering plenty of places to sit, although there are distractions like a huge TV screen, juke box and pool table. They go mad during the annual Boot beer festival at which they shift tens of different beers – at other times it's primarily a Robinson's house with up to three beers on handpump.

Leaving the pub, retrace your steps for a few yards past the white cottage and take the signed bridleway which runs very pleasantly in the trees alongside the beck for few yards with views across to the waterwheel of the mill. Take the path signed through a wall (it's such a ridiculously

tight squeeze that you may end up having to climb rather go through the wall) to the Hollins camp site. Skirt the top of the camp site and through the heavily suburbanised 'farmyard' which doesn't look as if it's seen an animal for many years, through a couple of fields via stiles which brings you on to a farm lane. Turn left here and walk up to the next house, Paddock Wray (B, ⊙, 184013). The exit from the field beyond it needs care in locating: make for the bottom right-hand corner of the rectangular field and a few yards up from this by an oak tree you should find a step stile marked with a white post. Now just follow the path to the left for a few yards to exit onto a small lane ahead of you. Turn right and simply walk down this lane to join the main Eskdale road, which is usually very quiet. From here it's just a few minutes walk left along the road before you'll reach the pleasantly-sited **Woolpack Inn 2**.

Now reopened under enthusiastic new managers, who have moved up the valley from the Boot Inn, the attached brewery is closed for the time being, but there's no shortage of beers on offer. There are up to eight to choose from, with the emphasis firmly upon Cumbria and northern England. Good-looking food is served all day until 9pm. The refurbished bar room looks a little stark at the moment but give them time. The place occupies a great setting and has a very pleasant front garden; if you like the sound of all this, it even offers

Blea Tarn

LEFT: **Brook House Inn** RIGHT: **Plenty of interesting choice at the Woolpack**

accommodation and they aim to 'go green' with their carbon footprint, according to the website...

Leaving the Woolpack retrace your steps for 150 yards to the signed lane on the left leading to Penny Hill Farm. Walk down this little tarred track which runs down to the river and then it's simply a question of following the riverside route which becomes a footpath at Doctor Bridge (don't cross). It's really a most attractive path with some open woodland and pleasant views through the trees.

It presently leaves the immediate riverside at a bit of a junction (but don't take the permitted path to Eel Tarn) and becomes more pronounced alongside a wall with good views across to the crags on the opposite bank.

Before long you'll reach St Catherine's Church, the parish church of Eskdale, sitting in an isolated location right on the river bank with the big fells of the Scafell group forming a backdrop. St Catherine's dates back to the 12th century when the Priory of St Bees owned a chapel here. Apart from good stained glass windows the octagonal font carries decorative marigold designs of the type found on Roman alters and early Christian tombstones.

There's a set of stepping stones across the river here; if you've time, you should consider the short detour to Stanley Ghyll Force waterfall; a 60-foot high waterfall in a dramatic deep and narrow gorge, but be warned that care is needed in places, as the path is very steep and unfenced.

Back at the church, the track veers away from the river at right angles; keep on the stony path and you'll see the big a three-storey white building straight ahead of you. That is our last stop of the day, the **Brook House Inn** 🛈, and it's simply a matter of following the track which emerges right opposite the pub.

This friendly and well-run family free house gets most things right on the food and drink front and has an extensive array of CAMRA, AA and RAC awards to show for it, notably the local CAMRA branch Pub of the Year award for 2010 – no mean feat with so much strong competition. Beer-wise, regulars Hawkshead Bitter and Taylor Landlord are supported by up to five rotating guests in the high season including some interesting 'outsiders' as well as locals like Yates and Jennings. It's not in every pub you come across a beer called Dr. Morton's Invisible Paint, for example! Aside from the attractive garden, there's a smaller room called the snug leading off the bar, and a separate dining room – the house policy means you can't book tables in the bar room during the busy evening period, so 'mere' drinkers are made to feel welcome.

Leaving the pub it's only a couple of minutes walk to the right along the road down to the Dalegarth rail terminus of the Ratty, and Beckfoot is seven or eight minutes further along beyond this if you've left the car there.

PUB INFORMATION

1 **Boot Inn**
Boot, Eskdale, CA19 1TG
01946 723224
www.bootinn.co.uk
Opening Hours: 11-11

2 **Woolpack Inn**
Eskdale, Holmrook
CA19 1TH
01946 723230
www.woolpack.co.uk
Opening Hours: 11-11; 12-10.30 Sun

3 **Brook House Inn**
Boot, Eskdale, CA19 1TG
019467 23288
www.brookhouseinn.co.uk
Opening Hours: 10 - midnight

▶ **LINK** ◀ A link path (p32) enables you to walk over via the shoulder of Harter Fell into the Duddon Valley close to the Newfield Inn at Seathwaite on walk 5.

RIGHT: **Up the Esk towards the Bowfell group of hills**

Link path: Eskdale to Duddon Valley

This easy-to-follow route will enable the fitter drinking walker to traverse fairly quickly from Eskdale and the **Woolpack Inn** [1] into the Duddon Valley (or Dunnerdale to give it its alternative name) for the **Newfield Inn** [2] in two or three hours – and taken together with the equally simple path joining Dunnerdale to Broughton, opens up several days of car-free walking and drinking! There's also the possibility of taking in an ascent of Harter Fell, for which either the Ordnance Survey map and/or a copy of Mr Wainwright's *Southern Fells* guide or similar; and a compass should be carried. The top section can get boggy so as usual pay attention to suitable footwear.

then pick out the less distinct path running up by the wall which climbs quite steeply to join the main path at A (see map).

The route up the fell bears up to the left hereabouts but the path to Dunnerdale is the well-trodden highway towards the obvious col (pass) following the stream uphill, on which you'll soon reach the wide (and in wetter conditions rather boggy) summit area close to a broken wall which runs up to the summit of Harter Fell on your left. The view in front is of a far more wooded valley where the recent felling and replanting of conifer plantations makes for a changing scene, but the track carries on downhill (take the right fork in a few minutes which drops steadily down) towards Grassguards, picking up the stream, the Grassguards Gill, very shortly.

Competent map readers can keep on the right-hand bank of the stream at Grassguards and take the good bridleway to High Wallowbarrow and thence to the footbridge to Seathwaite – but to avoid any confusion it's easier perhaps to take the left fork at Grassguards, cross the Gill, and walk steadily downhill, following the stream, to meet the riverside path (B, ⊙ 228975), at which point simply follow the stream to the right as per walk 5, to emerge by the

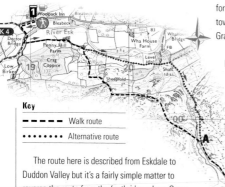

Key
– – – – Walk route
• • • • • • Alternative route

The route here is described from Eskdale to Duddon Valley but it's a fairly simple matter to reverse the route from the footbridge where Grassguards Gill meets the Duddon River at B.

From the Woolpack follow the instructions for walk 4 as far as Doctor Bridge, but in this case cross the bridge and take the bridleway left for Penny Hill Farm. Pass through the farm and continue to the group of buildings some 200 yards beyond, where a path on a track bears right up the hill, over the first wall and then veers left through another to keep above the walled enclosures and the steeper ground to your right. Follow it round to the right a little as it crosses a small stream and then joins the larger path which comes up from the foot of Hardknott Pass by Spothow Gill (A, ⊙ 207998). The views of Eskdale on this stretch are excellent and the colours very varied, especially in autumn.

An alternative is to continue on the Bridleway from Penny Hill for a further half a mile until you reach the Spothow Gill, where a good path drops back down to the road at Wha House Farm – and

footbridges into Seathwaite and the Newfield Inn in about half an hour.

Tackling the route in reverse there should be no difficulties except you may miss the path veering off to the left at A, but it's not a problem to continue down the gill along the wall and either join the bridleway to Penny Hill and Doctor Bridge, or indeed simply to go right down to the road at Wha House and turn left for the Woolpack. Consult your map!

Duddon Valley

WALK 5

WALK INFORMATION

Start/Finish: Birks Bridge car park (235994); or Seathwaite, adjacent Newfield Inn

Access: No public transport. Possible to walk in from Eskdale or Broughton Mills (see link routes, pages 32 and 44)

Distance: 6 miles (9.7km)

OS map: OS Explorer OL6

Key attractions: Peaceful valley; optional walk to Seathwaite Tarn

The pubs: Newfield Inn, Seathwaite

Widely-regarded as the quietest of the larger Lakeland valleys, the Duddon Valley (or Dunnerdale as it's also known) is difficult to get to, protected in the north to an extent by the two steep passes of Hardknott and Wrynose, and with only a narrow twisting lane running down the valley which has few settlements of any size. The characterful Newfield Inn is very much the social hub of the valley and enables the scenery to be enjoyed without being too far from a welcome pint. Moreover, there are straightforward link walks to north and south linking this valley both with Eskdale and Broughton in Furness, so drinking backpackers can combine several routes in this book either side of shy Dunnerdale. Although the walk as described here starts and finishes at Birks Bridge car park, it's a very plausible alternative to start in Seathwaite by the pub, although bear in mind that the full circuit will take at least three hours, maybe more, so it may depend on what time you arrive to start.

Cottage nestled under the rocks in the Duddon Valley

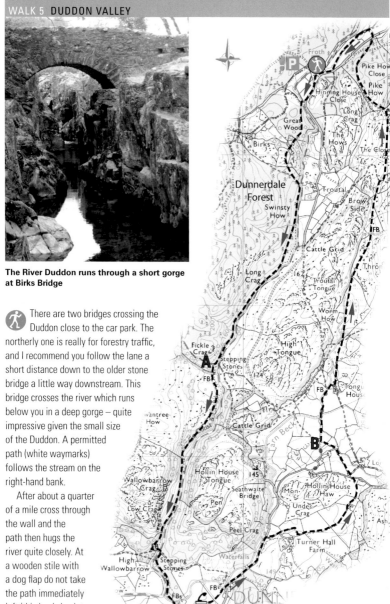

The River Duddon runs through a short gorge at Birks Bridge

There are two bridges crossing the Duddon close to the car park. The northerly one is really for forestry traffic, and I recommend you follow the lane a short distance down to the older stone bridge a little way downstream. This bridge crosses the river which runs below you in a deep gorge – quite impressive given the small size of the Duddon. A permitted path (white waymarks) follows the stream on the right-hand bank.

After about a quarter of a mile cross through the wall and the path then hugs the river quite closely. At a wooden stile with a dog flap do not take the path immediately left (this leads back to the river but ends at an impasse), but go over the stile and you'll spot the waymark above the wall. Pick up the path up through the trees which leads up onto a rocky knoll. At the little summit there are good views, Harter Fell on your right, the Seathwaite fells looking towards Dow Crag on the left, and straight ahead Caw.

The path now drops back down towards the river though an area of quite dense birch woodland. Ignore the wooden footbridge to continue on the right-hand bank, in turn through coniferous and deciduous woodland, crossing a small side stream by a high waterfall with flood damage much in evidence. Cross a tributary by a wire footbridge where the bridleway to Grassguards and Eskdale (A,  228976 – see link path, page 32) leads up the valley to your right, and now you're on your last mile before welcome refreshment. Pass under the impressive Wallowbarrow screes before finally descending back down to the riverside. From here its just another 200 yards or so to the footbridge which we take to cross the river Duddon, and taking the path through the trees close to the river, you come out on the little valley road once again. Its now only couple of minutes' walk to the right before you arrive at the **Newfield Inn** 1.

Newfield Inn, Seathwaite

It's a fine old building done out in white render and set back a wee bit from the lane which makes a dog-leg through the little hamlet of Seathwaite. The atmospheric interior is tailor-made for the thirsty walker: no plush carpets with unwelcome invitations to remove your boots here! Indeed, the Newfield is blessed with what must be the best floor of a Lakeland pub – huge slabs of well-worn striped Walna Scar slate. Like so many other old pubs, the venerable old building has been opened out to a large extent but still retains character and some semblance of separate areas. To the rear there's a pleasant garden complete with childrens' play area. Beers are Jennings Cumberland Ale plus one or more guests, whilst food is served all day – useful to know if you're arriving here mid-afternoon after doing the whole circuit.

Leaving the Newfield, look out for the footpath right opposite the pub which leads across the meadow and cuts the corner off the road – which you rejoin through a stile at the far right-hand corner of the field (disregard the other path leading back down to the river and footbridge). Follow the quiet lane along the valley for about 450 yards; if you wish, avoid the road for a couple of hundred yards by diverting into a riverside path at the small lay-by.

Turn right onto the public footpath at the Turner Hall camp site sign and follow the well-marked route on a stony track which runs into

Across the Dunnerdale Fells

Harter Fell rises above the woodland of the Duddon Valley

walled fell country through a couple of gates. Reach the first house and pass through the gate following the line of telegraph wires (disregard the ladder stile over to your right). Follow the waymarks across a lane and past another house and downhill following a well-marked route through the bottom gate in the field to join the tarmac lane (B, 235971).

Turn right here, and ignoring the sign left by the bridge, follow the lane to Tongue House where at the whitewashed cottage take the marked path sharp left by the green entrance gate. Now simply follow in more or less the same direction for the best part of a mile as the route climbs up to a col (or pass) in what feels like a more remote spot than it really is. Over a ladder stile, keeping the stream on your left, and follow the stream with telegraph poles as your companion, to the col ahead.

Eventually you cross the stream on a footbridge and continuing up slightly more steeply now to the top of col, aiming directly ahead towards the conifer trees. The path now runs close to the wall

up on your right. At this point, fit and ambitious walkers might wish to detour up the fellside to visit Seathwaite Reservoir above, but do consult a map and/or suitable guide book.

Otherwise or afterwards, continue ahead into the grassy valley following the right-hand fork of the telegraph wires into a conifer woodland ahead, following clear waymarks up a rather steep pull and over the wooded knoll into the upper Duddon Valley to reach the valley road again just short of Hinning House, the prominent building ahead of you. Look out for tiny cars apparently coming down the mountain side in the distance: this is Hardknott Pass, England's most tortuous fell road. The path emerges by a footpath sign and almost opposite is another leading down into the riverside meadow. Take this and follow it as it swings left so you're walking downstream with the river on your right. You emerge onto the road again just short of the Birks Bridge car park.

Walkers relaxing in the Newfield Inn, Seathwaite

PUB INFORMATION

1 Newfield Inn
Seathwaite, LA20 6ED
01229 716208
www.newfieldinn.co.uk
Opening Hours: 11-11;
12-11 Sun

▶ **LINK** See p32 for a link path from the Newfield Inn to the Woolpack, Eskdale (walk 4), or p44 for a link path to the Blacksmiths Arms, Broughton Mills (walk 6).

Furness Group –
the South West

Woodland on the shore of Coniston Water

Broughton beer tour

WALK 6

WALK INFORMATION

Start/Finish: Broughton in Furness

Access: Bus 511 Broughton–Ulverston. Trains from Foxfield

Distance: Circuit from Broughton in Furness via Blacksmith's Arms 5.9 miles (9.5km). Foxfield extension 1.8 miles (3km)

OS map: OS Explorer OL6

Key attractions: Historic Broughton in Furness; Blacksmiths Arms pub; Duddon ironworks; Duddon bridge (GR 197882)

The pubs: Blacksmiths Arms, Broughton Mills; Manor Arms, Black Cock, both Broughton; Prince of Wales, Foxfield. Try also: Old Kings Head, Broughton

There can be few more attractive small towns in Cumbria than Broughton in Furness. With a history going back a millennium, it was once an important market town. Today pride of place goes to its elegant Georgian square fringed with merchants' houses. The walk consists of a circuit from the town through the pleasant rural landscape to the north calling at the atmospheric Blacksmiths Arms, listed on CAMRA's National Inventory of heritage pubs. In addition, there's a short walk between Broughton and the excellent Prince of Wales adjacent Foxfield station, which is not to be missed by beer lovers. The walking is not strenuous and the navigation not overly complex but you need to pay heed to the map to avoid going astray in some places. Note the closure of the Prince of Wales at the beginning of the week, and plan accordingly! The Broughton beer festival takes place each November.

The Manor Arms stands right on Broughton's town square

The walk starts at Broughton, by the Obelisk (constructed to mark the Jubilee of King George III in 1810) in the market square; if you arrive at Foxfield station, see below for the route into Broughton.

Leave Broughton town square by the north-east corner (up the hill from the Manor Arms), and walking up towards the small park and the public conveniences bear right for about a hundred yards and join a bridleway signed 'Woodland 1¼ miles'. This is the track bed of the former railway line which ran from the junction at Foxfield up to Coniston. For an old railway the gradient is quite steep as it rises out of town, fringed these days with rhododendrons.

Follow this route under a bridge, just beyond which there are a couple of ponds on your left with a bench which makes a good spot for a breather. In another half a mile cross a trackway and about a hundred yards beyond this look out for a gateway on the left – this leads straight onto another path rising steadily away from the old rail track bed, a pleasant route enclosed (when you gain some height) between walls with good views opening out towards the Coniston fells. The route levels off once you've passed through a gate and turned right following the obvious track along the contour with woodland on your left and good views on your right.

Reach the Coniston road (A, ⊕ 228896) and cross carefully more or less directly opposite onto a track which is a mixture of grass and tarmac. This twists and turns uphill reaching the entrance to Wallenrigg Farm where the surface improves and leads you, still climbing gently, to reach a T-junction in another few minutes. At about 350 feet this is the highest point of the walk, lying on a long ridge running between two valleys.

It's all downhill to the pub now, but a bit of care is needed to find the correct line: about 10 yards to the right of the T-junction the path we're after leads off into a field on the left – follow the field boundary to your left down, and at the bottom of the field bear left over the stile and walk along the boundary of the next field. In about 75 yards, where the field boundary starts climbing uphill, look for a path down into the trees over a gate and then follow the line of trees down through two metal gates. Once over the second

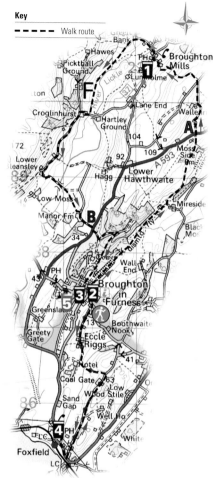

Key
– – – – – Walk route

gate bear half left downhill towards a line of trees and again follow the field boundary using the mature trees and some large boulders as a marker until you're able to identify a stile at the foot of the field, almost hidden in the trees. Once over this, follow the now more obvious path around the building and down the access lane to join the minor road at Broughton Mills, whereupon the **Blacksmiths Arms** 🛑 is a mere 75 yards or so to the left.

This isolated but nonetheless well-known pub is well worth the navigational effort in reaching it. Externally it's a handsome and solid 18th-century house, and it has arguably the most unspoilt interior of any Lakeland hostelry. Stone floors and

The bar room at the Blacksmiths Arms

wooden benches are the welcome order of the day, and the basic public bar has an open fire as one might expect. The Blacksmiths offers three changing beers, usually Jennings Cumberland plus two rotating locally-brewed guests; and Foxfield cider. Happily, the extensive food menu served in the adjacent dining room is not at the expense of the character of the room, unlike many other pubs. In good weather there's a small but pleasant patio area at the front of the pub where you can admire the architecture in its setting whilst you sup your pint.

Leaving the pub, retrace your steps to and past the footpath where you emerged onto the road, and bear left at the road junction just beyond. Turn left again just over the stream where the main road turns sharply right for Ulpha, and walk up to the little hamlet of Green Bank. Find and follow the signed footpath leading left through

the farm gate passing the very impressive old vernacular barn and through another gate onto a stony track with wide views out down the valley and towards the coast.

This next stretch is a pleasant walk along the valley floor. Keep close to the stream, avoiding any paths rising up the hill to the right. In a little over half a mile from Green Bank you'll emerge onto a tarred lane where you turn right, and follow the road as it zigzags up through the tiny hamlet of Croglinhurst, before swinging left to run more or less south towards Middle Bleansley Farm and then Lower Bleansley. Here the tarmac runs out but the right of way drops down the farm track to your left curving around and running down to the river which it crosses on this good track. Follow the track up towards Manor Farm ahead of you, looking out for the stile just before reaching the buildings which takes you up onto the lane above the farm. Join this and turn right following the farm track to join the main road (B, 214884).

Almost opposite you are a set of locked gates which look impregnable, but on closer inspection there's a new stone stile on the left of the embayment, reassuringly signed 'public footpath'. This enables you to pass into the estate and follow the fence up towards the house (which is now a

The tiny hamlet of Foxfield lies on the coast by Duddon Sands

school). At the locked gates here bear 90-degrees left along the boundary climbing up for about 350 yards whereupon double sharply back to your right on another path on a prominent ridge with good views over to your left looking down onto the first part of the route and the lakes we passed earlier. Follow the line with the house on the right to a stile at the top of a field, through a couple more stiles and out to the town square at Broughton where we started. Its certain that by now you'll be in the mood to appreciate the **Manor Arms** 2 located in an enviable spot overlooking the charming square.

This is a pub which deserves all the superlatives which it gets, with committed staff ensuring that the wide range of ales are in very good condition. Expect a beer from Skipton's Copper Dragon and the popular Yates Bitter plus as many as six changing guests. The opened-out interior nonetheless retains plenty of character and there are several little corners you can settle into for a decent session if you wish. Food isn't served here but help is at hand if you want to eat in Broughton: make your way down past the Town House (now the Tourist Information office) to the lower corner of the square, and turn left onto Griffin Street and left again into Princes Street. Here, with one of the finest pub signs in Cumbria, lies the old **Black Cock** 3. This 16th-century inn is a characterful gem with genuine old oak

beams and thick walls. There's also a secluded little patio garden at the rear. Alongside regulars Marston's Pedigree and Theakston Best expect up to three rotating guests, maybe from new micro Lancaster whose Black stout was in good form on my last visit. Food is served daily until 9pm.

If you're going to stay here in Broughton for the night (and all the town's pubs and inns offer accommodation) you could try the **Old Kings Head** 5, further down Griffin Street. However, no committed beer drinker would want to miss the Prince of Wales overlooking Duddon Sands, so either to round off a superlative day's walking and imbibing, or the following day, you need to make your way down there; a distance on foot of just over a mile.

From the market square adjacent to the Manor Arms, head east along Market Street and follow the road down then uphill to the top opposite the primary school where there's a turning to the right (footpath sign). Follow this gently uphill with good views across the town; disregard the first footpath sign left by a small hamlet after about a quarter of a mile. Instead continue past a couple more cottages and the path then veers slightly to the left of the Millers Cottage through a gate and out into an extensive field with fine views over Eccleriggs. Keep well to the left of the large country house which you can see in front of you and aim straight ahead through a gate where you'll see a post by a large pine tree – this is the line of the right of way. Look now for the Cumbria Coastal Way signs which leads you down across a golf fairway to the valley floor, across a small footbridge and uphill on a well-signed section through a couple of stiles to join the tarmac road. Now, turning right it's a simply a matter of following this track which runs along the low ridge for

The National Inventory-listed Blacksmiths Arms at Broughton Mills

LEFT: **Possibly the best pub sign in Lakeland?**   RIGHT: **The Prince of Wales is handy for the train**

about half a mile to join the main road at Foxfield. As you might expect there are wide views out over the Duddon Sands, the small bay ahead, and the wider Furness coastline.

When you reach the main road bear right and follow the road as it runs along close to the railway line for about 200 yards. Now right by the railway station is the welcoming sight of the **Prince of Wales 4**, and there can be few better places to hole up after a long day's walking than the Prince with its renowned selection of beers and attractive menu. The guv'nor and his wife acquired the pub some fifteen years ago and set up a small brewery here turning out a variety of differing ales whilst often offering something from their their previous enterprise: the Tigertops brewery in Wakefield. In addition there are up to six changing guests with all sorts of interesting and unusual brews apt to turn up. The food is excellent and enjoyed by all, alongside the snacks which often appear in bowls on the bar. Service is attentive, and it's worth mentioning in an area where short measure is not uncommon that the Prince uses lined glasses. All in all, it's no wonder aficionados make good use of the rail service to visit the pub on a regular basis, particularly for the local folk sessions on Wednesday evening. You have the option of booking ahead one of the pub's bedrooms if you want to make a night of it: a generous discount is offered for members of CAMRA.

If you are arriving by train and starting the route at Foxfield before making for Broughton, simply turn left out the pub (right from the station level crossing) and walk down to the road junction to turn left and take in the long straight rising lane. Look out for the Cumbria Coastal Way sign after about half a mile, which then leads you clearly down across the golf course curving up keeping the large hotel on your left and join the little lane by the Millers Cottage where you bear right and follow the lane straight down into Broughton by the primary school and turn left down into the town centre at the Manor Arms.

PUB INFORMATION

1 Blacksmiths Arms
Broughton Mills, LA20 6AX
01229 716824
www.theblacksmithsarms.com
Opening Hours: 12-2.30 (not Mon), 5-11; 12-11 Sat; 12-10.30 Sun; summer 12 (5 Mon)-11; 12-10.30 Sun

2 Manor Arms
The Square, Broughton in Furness, LA20 6HY
01229 716286
www.manorarmsthesquare.co.uk
Opening Hours: 12-11.30 (midnight Fri & Sat); 12-11 Sun

3 Black Cock
Princes Street, Broughton in Furness, LA20 6HQ
01229 716529
www.blackcockinncumbria.com
Opening Hours: 12 (12.30 Sun)-11 (midnight Wed & Thu; 1am Fri & Sat)

4 Prince of Wales
Foxfield, LA20 6BX
01229 716238
www.princeofwalesfoxfield.co.uk
Opening Hours: 12 (2.45 Wed & Thu)-11 (10.30 Sun); closed Mon & Tue

TRY ALSO:

5 Old Kings Head
Church Street, Broughton in Furness, LA20 6HJ
01229 716293
www.oldkingshead.co.uk
Opening Hours: 12-11 (midnight Fri & Sat)

LINK   see p44 for a link path from the Blacksmiths Arms to the Newfield Inn, Seathwaite (walk 5).

Link path: Duddon Valley to Broughton Mills

If you're a hardy backpacking drinker and/or you're staying in either the Duddon Valley or around Broughton then the route described here, through the Dunnerdale Fells, is a very good link path enabling you to connect two excellent Lakeland pubs: the **Newfield Inn** in Seathwaite with the **Blacksmiths Arms** at Broughton Mills. Keep an eye on the weather though, as the bridleway rises to around 1,000 feet and the central section can

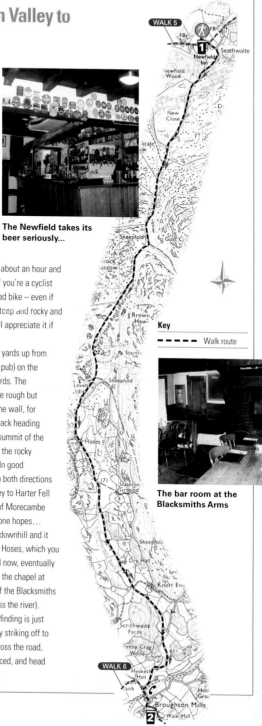

The Newfield takes its beer seriously...

be exposed in wild conditions. Allow about an hour and a half to do the three mile traverse. If you're a cyclist this is a very good route for an off-road bike – even if the first section from Seathwaite is steep and rocky and you may have to push your bike, you'll appreciate it if seeking to return later in the day.

The bridleway is signed just a few yards up from the Newfield Inn (turn right out of the pub) on the corner where the road bends northwards. The instructions are very simple: follow the rough but well-marked bridleway uphill, along the wall, for about a mile, whereupon ignore the track heading off left and continue ahead up to the summit of the path through a distinct col (pass) with the rocky outcrop of Brock Barrow on the right. In good weather a superb view can be head in both directions – northwards across the Duddon Valley to Harter Fell and south down to the sand and sea of Morecambe Bay, bathed in shimmering sunshine, one hopes...

The path is equally easy to follow downhill and it joins the road just above the house at Hoses, which you pass on the way, relentlessly downhill now, eventually crossing the little River Lickle close to the chapel at Hesketh Hall, just a few yards north of the Blacksmiths Arms (turn right at the T-junction across the river).

In the opposite direction the route finding is just as easy: just look out for the bridleway striking off to the right beyond Hoses and a gate across the road, where the tarred road becomes unfenced, and head up to the col and over.

Key

– – – – Walk route

The bar room at the Blacksmiths Arms

Haverthwaite & the Leven Valley

WALK INFORMATION

Start/Finish: Haverthwaite station

Access: By lake launch from Bowness to Lakeside pier then Lakeside & Haverthwaite Railway; bus X35 Kendal to Barrow stops outside station

Distance: Whole circuit: 6.6 miles (10.6km); eastern circuit via Backbarrow: 3.2 miles (5.2km)

OS map: OS Explorer OL7

Key attractions: Lakeside & Haverthwaite Railway; Stott Park Bobbin Mill, Newby Bridge; Aquarium of the Lakes, Haverthwaite; Lakeland Motor Museum, Backbarrow; woodland and estuarine habitats

The pubs: Anglers Arms, Haverthwaite

Plenty of variety is on offer on this easy walk along the Leven Valley. For railway enthusiasts it's a must, although the trains only run April–October, so I recommend that you do this walk in summer. Even if you don't arrive by boat and rail at the start, Haverthwaite is an attractive old station with an excellent platform buffet serving snacks and meals. The walk is arranged as a figure of eight – the first half is through some well-wooded landscape with good views into the valley; the second follows the lower reaches of the river valley. You can either do both the loops, with a visit to the pub in the middle, or just do one of the loops and relax thereafter. Naturally, if you're relying on the train to return you to Lakeside for the Bowness launch, plan ahead with the timetable. Be warned that the A590 road which you need to cross three times is fast and unpleasant – you'll need your wits about you.

Lakeside & Haverthwaite Railway

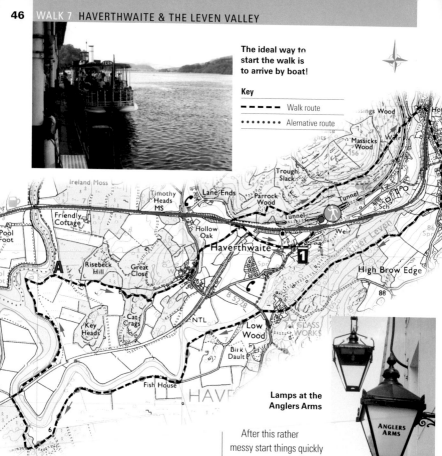

The ideal way to start the walk is to arrive by boat!

Key

– – – – Walk route

• • • • • • Alernative route

Lamps at the
Anglers Arms

Start at Haverthwaite station, where a pot of tea will get things off to a good start. Walk down to the busy main road and cross with care. Use the signed crossing a few yards along to the left and be aware of the speed of traffic. Walk down the lane opposite where you'll see the Angler's Arms about 150 yards away. Walk past the pub keeping it on your left, go through a couple of gates, and there's a signpost and a stile in the wall on the right, above the new road. Go through the stile and walk, rather unsatisfactorily, along the other side of the wall squeezing past the vegetation, until the path drops down to the roadside. Again take great care crossing, as the traffic is very fast and won't be expecting you. Opposite, you're faced with a rather undignified scramble up about 15 feet of bank to the narrow lane by the wall above, with a gate on the right ('permitted path to Backbarrow').

After this rather messy start things quickly improve. After about 200 yards take the right-hand fork, and follow the waymark to the right shortly afterwards. Then it's a case of following the clear track as it winds up and down through the attractive woodlands, carpeted with blubells and wild garlic in spring. Eventually reach a waymark at a junction of paths and take the right-hand, Backbarrow, route. Five minutes later take the uphill, left-hand fork in the paths and then right at the next fork which leads downhill and out to a road through a narrow bridge under the railway line. This is Backbarrow. It ought to be less complicated than it sounds!

You've emerged at a point where ahead of you a bridge crosses the river on a large weir. The Whitewater Hotel here has been converted from a former mill building. Backbarrow was once an important industrial centre (see box) by virtue of the fast flowing River Leven making its way down from Lake Windermere (which is about 130 feet (40 metres) above sea level) to the estuary. A good deal of that height was lost in the narrow gorge where we're now standing, and there were mills and an iron foundry here. Backbarrow Cotton Mill was notorious for its bad treatment of the children who worked there. Later, it was to become an ultramarine works (see box), when water all around it was coloured blue. Backbarrow also had an ironworks, one of the oldest in the country.

Cross the river, noting evidence of the damage caused by the November 2009 floods which ripped down walls and badly damaged the hotel and the road bridge itself, as well as sweeping away the footbridge downstream. Take the first turning right which becomes a footpath leading up to the busy main road. Cross the road carefully by the traffic island, and take the first turning left, Brow Edge Road. You walk up here quite a way, climbing the whole time, and ignoring a signed footpath before, in a few minutes, taking a bridleway, once again with a clear new finger post, which

Lakeside & Haverthwaite Railway

heads off to the right. The reward for the climb through this rather nondescript residential road is far-reaching views for the modest height, including views across to the wooded Haverthwaite heights across the valley, and down to the railway station. This bridleway is one of the highpoints of the walk, with wild flowers and good tree cover complementing the fine views. It's also steadily downhill; you'll have to put up with the drone of vehicles speeding along the road, however. Watch out for some old industrial remains in the woods on the right lower down.

INDUSTRY AT BACKBARROW

Backbarrow had been an important industrial site for several hundred years on account of the fast flowing river Leven. The monks of Cartmel Abbey operated a corn mill here, and later both fulling and paper mills were sited here, although these were superseded by the notorious cotton mill. It was investigated by the Parliamentary commission in 1816, on account of harsh conditions under which apprentices were engaged. It was gutted in a severe fire in 1868 and was never reopened.

The 'Blue Mill' came later: Ultramarine in its natural state is a gemstone called lapis lazuli, which even in biblical times was used as decoration and adornment by the wealthy. Later a vivid blue paint was manufactured by mixing ground

The lower part of the walk follows the River Leven

lapis lazuli with oils and beeswax; and when the Saracens invaded Byzantium and the natives fled to the West, they brought with them the knowledge and evidence of the vivid blue. Older readers may remember 'Dolly Blue' or 'Reckitts Blue' after the manufacturer – which was used as an additive in washing machines to keep shirts looking white before modern detergents. There's an information panel about this in the motor museum.

John Wilkinson was well known during the industrial revolution for his involvement in the iron works and eventually garnered the title 'Iron Mad John' for his experiments with using iron in unconventional ways. He even made his coffin out of iron. His father, Isaac, who taught him the skills necessary for ironworking worked at the Backbarrow Ironworks foundry.

LEFT: **The bridleway after leaving Backbarrow** RIGHT: **Anglers Arms**

In about two thirds of a mile you emerge on a lower road which brings you quickly to a river bridge. Opposite here a tarred cycleway continues along the riverside – this is the continuation of the walk. However, if you wish to detour to the Anglers Arms or cut the walk short, this is the point at which to do so. To get to the pub, cross the river and immediately take the footpath on the right. In 250 yards this emerges via a yard onto a quiet road. Turn right and follow it up to the pub. The **Anglers Arms** 1 offers a wide range of up to eight ales from near and far; and a draught cider. There are two spacious bars, and the public bar has a pool table on a lower level. The reasonably-priced food is well regarded.

Allow a couple of hours for the lower loop of the route if you wish to continue your walk. Retrace your steps to the start of the riverside cycleway (don't miss the left turn onto the footpath by the buildings). Follow this lane and veer right onto a signed riverside footpath after 200 yards. A pleasant stretch brings you back to the same lane a short distance later – then in this suddenly very flat landscape its an uneventful half a mile or so following the private road (but public path). Shortly after entering the woodland (just after crossing a stream) there's a clear signpost off to the right. Things improve scenically, and a pleasant wooded path leads you to an abandoned railway trackbed, where the path makes use of the old railway bridge to cross the now rather wider river Leven. Once over the river bear left and follow the meandering river, with a distinctly coastal feel now,

for half a mile, keeping on the river embankment until you leave the Leven and turn up the Rusland Valley, and arrive at a signpost and stile running inland from the riverside embankment (A, ⊙, 331838). You'll know you're at the correct place since about 400 yards away you'll spot the main road crossing the river on a modern bridge.

The inland path which we take here passes by a telegraph pole and beyond a gate, a large tree. The last section of the walk changes character again now traversing some mature woodland – but don't let yourself get drawn off course by the forest track which leads round the right-hand stand of trees – rather, keep towards the left-hand tree belt across the field and you'll shortly arrive at a waymark by a gate into the trees. Bear right as the path winds uphill through the woodland before dropping again into a little hidden valley which in turn brings you out into a small settle-ment. The trick here is to keep ahead through the narrow lane and merge with the main B5278 road, bearing left. Opposite, a few yards ahead at the end of the retaining wall along the road, a signed path leads down into a vale and up to the point, which you'll recognise from then start of the walk, where the step stile leads through the wall above the dual carriageway. So it's just a case of turning right back through the kissing gate and retracing your steps to the Anglers Arms. Buses will take you to Kendal or Ulverston if you want to spend the evening in town.

PUB INFORMATION

1 Anglers Arms
Old Barrow Road, Haverthwaite,
LA12 8AJ
01539 531216
mj7trina@aol.com
Opening Hours: 11.30-midnight;
11.30-1am Sat; 12-midnight Sun

▶ LINK ◀ Take the X35 bus to Kendal (walks 15 and 19), 15 miles; and to Ulverston (walk 10), 6 miles.

A Coniston & Torver circuit

WALK INFORMATION

Start/Finish: Coniston village

Access: Blueworks service X12 Ulverston (for railway) to Coniston; summer buses 505 from Windermere & Ambleside

Distance: 6 miles (9.7km)

OS map: OS Explorer OL5

Key attractions: Coniston water and village; steam yacht trips in summer; hill walks from Coniston; John Ruskin's grave and Ruskin museum; Brantwood, Ruskin's lakeside house (2 miles)

The pubs: Church House Inn, Torver; Black Bull, Sun, both Coniston. Try also: Ship, Bowmanstead

Pleasantly sited on the shore of Coniston Water, which at five miles long and with a maximum depth of 184 feet, is the third largest of the lakes, the village of Coniston is a deservedly popular place with visitors. Like many other modern beauty spots in the national park it wasn't always a mere tourist trap: the valley running down from the mountains behind the village was once the scene of several active copper and slate mines, while the lake was a significant source of fish for the monks of Furness Abbey. All of the pubs in this pleasant walk offer a wide range of guest beers so there should be plenty to choose from for even the thirstiest walker. Navigation along the inland leg from Coniston needs some care, and there is an initial very steep climb, albeit on tarmac!

The Black Bull, Coniston

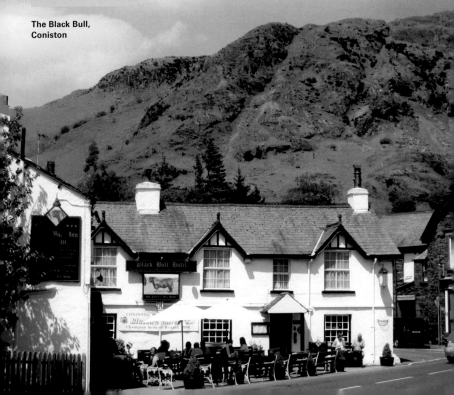

Cumbria Way path alongside
Coniston Water

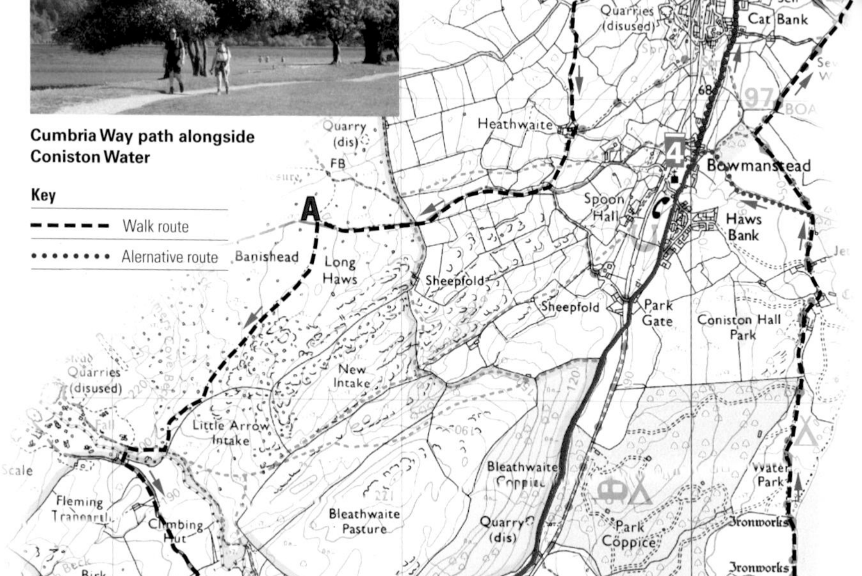

Key
– – – – Walk route
• • • • • • Alternative route

Start in the centre of Coniston by the river bridge. For many older readers Coniston will forever be associated with Donald Campbell, who died in 1967 after successfully reaching over 300mph on the lake in his craft *Bluebird* as he tried to better his own world record for water speed. His father had himself claimed the then world record at 141mph on the lake in 1939. There is a memorial to him near the Information Centre in Ruskin Avenue, and the story is told in greater detail in the Ruskin Museum. The flagship beer of the local Coniston brewery commemorates Campbell's jet-powered boat, and you can try the full range of Coniston beers in the Black Bull right in the centre of the village.

A lane immediately south of the bridge (across the river from the Black Bull) leads up towards the Sun Hotel and Inn (which like the Black Bull I suggest you save for later: the first mile or so of navigation requires a bit of concentration!).

The road bears left in front of the Sun (ignore the footpath immediately beyond the pub) and meets a junction where you should take the road to the right. Now, let yourself be guided by the primary white road markings to follow the road steeply uphill (signed 'Walna Scar'). This is the start of the ancient route over to the Duddon Valley. You'll know you're on the right road as you will be walking up a remarkably steep, tarred, tree-lined lane which quickly gives rewarding views across to the Coppermines Valley – and you'll have earnt them in full measure.

At the top of this steep toil have a well-deserved rest where the road bends 90-degrees left, but don't follow the dog leg round to the right, rather, carry on ahead on the stony track through a gate and onto a path signed 'Heathwaite'. Carry on over the stile and along the clear track over the meadow and down towards the farm, as a fine view opens out over Coniston Water below you. There's a well-sited stone seat you can take advantage of. On the lake shore the prominent building with the signature circular chimneys is Coniston Hall, which we'll pass on the last leg of the walk later on. Carrying on down to Heathwaite ahead, where a couple of gates lead through the yard and out the far side (the map shows the path skirting around the farmyard but until they sign it clearly I would have no hesitation about the

direct route!) where we make for a third gate at the bottom of a short wall. Pass through here and contour across the next field (ignoring the stile on the right above you) to reach yet another gate by a stream, and beyond it a clear bridlepath turning right (uphill) along the side of the stream. Follow this path, thankfully not as steep as earlier, with fine views opening up ahead – Dow Crag is the fell emerging behind the Old Man of Coniston – and reach a ladder stile over the wall.

Disregard the crossing path and continue ahead onto the common. In about 5 minutes – at the top of the rise where the path levels out, and beside a small mere with a boulder set into the grass just beyond it – you'll see a rather indistinct path (looking more like a gulley) bearing off at right angles to the left (A, ⊕ 287966). This leads gently uphill towards the highest ground ahead. Bearing gently to the right to keep this flat summit on your left, head downhill, keeping slightly rocky ground to your left, so that you're walking towards an old quarry spoil tip ahead with walled meadows to the left of it. Soon a wall leads in from the left to meet you and at the foot of the slope, by a stream, you join a path emerging from a gate in that same wall. But rather than taking this path, bear right to cross the stream on a small wooden bridge and head for the gates beyond it at the foot of the spoil tips.

In a few yards cross a much larger stream on a footbridge and passing through three gates, bear

Coniston Hall and the lake from Heathwaite

The Old Man of Coniston is never far away...

left to pick up the wide track running downhill passing Tranearth cottage (a climbing hut). You can temporarily switch to auto pilot for the next mile or so as the good stony lane leads mostly downhill towards Torver. At Scarr Head the now tarred lane bears sharply left and then right: follow this round. To avoid the main road at the foot of the road, take the footpath a short way down on the right and you'll see Torver church across on your left. The **Church House Inn 1** is the white building immediately to its right. To get there leave this little walled lane as it curves right and cross the (at first hidden) stile to emerge via the lower field onto the road by another stile right opposite the pub.

Coniston Bluebird	3.6%
Hawkshead Bitter	3.7%
Kelham · Easy Rider	4.3%
Copper Dragon Golden Pippin	3.9%
Black Sheep	3.8%
Loweswater Gold	4.3%
Barngates Tag Lag	4.4%
Cumberland Corby Ale	3.8%
Coming Soon	
Yates Golden Ale	3.9%
Clark's Classic Blonde	3.9%
Purple Moose · Glaslyn Ale	4.2%
Dalesado Blonde	3.9%

It's co-owned by renowned chef Michael Beaty who has worked in some of the poshest eateries both here and in France. He was a one-time private chef to David Bowie (who still looks young while most of his contemporaries are dead or look like it) so you can be pretty sure the food will be good if you end up eating here. And the beer in this attractive and unusually-shaped pub won't let you down either: up to five changing local ales (with Barngates Tag Lag and a Hawkshead beer as regulars) are served from the sturdy bar resting on old wooden casks. A solid slate flag floor sets off the open fire very well. There's a separate and comfortable lounge, and dining room beyond. Outside is a particularly pleasant garden, and the service is friendly and helpful.

Care is required when leaving the Church House if it's the tourist season and the road is busy – for we want to turn right and walk back up to the river bridge and beyond where a footpath heads off to the right. Unfortunately there is no footpath for most of the way on the road. If you really don't fancy it, an alternative may be to walk the other way where there is path, and at the junction with the A5084 in 200 yards turn left onto this quieter 'A' road and follow it down (partial footpath) to the minor lane across the river (a 5 minute walk), and turn left along here to reach point B (see alternative route on map). On the main route, take the footpath (signed 'Torver Hill and lake'), and follow this down the side of the fence through stiles and gates to the tiny lane (B, ⊙ 288944). Cross this lane (or turn right if coming along it) towards Brackenbarrow Farm, along a pleasant path and just beyond the farm buildings fork right at a choice of routes keeping a wall on your right and a field to your left.

RIGHT: **Looking accross Coniston Water from the east shore to the village and the fells**

LEFT: **Church House Inn** RIGHT: **The Sun, Coniston**

As you enter a gate into Torver Commons you'll realise that you're still quite high up as you'll catch a glimpse of the lake quite a way below you. The charming path leads you down to the lake shore, following a lightly wooded valley, and soon you'll reach the lake itself by a new finger-board which points left on the Cumbria Way for Coniston. The first stretch of this easy path keeps right by the lake shore, and would make a good spot for a siesta if the weather permits.

The large house on the opposite shore in a clearing is Brantwood, once John Ruskin's home. Ruskin had close associations with this area as with others, and his museum is back in Coniston village. The Cumbria Way, well signed throughout, does depart a little from the lake shore after about half a mile, leading via the pleasantly sited camp site and up to Coniston Hall, an old house, possibly 16th-century, owned by the National Trust. It has some impressive circular chimney stacks, a feature of many fine old houses in the area.

Beyond the hall, the footpath bears right from the camp site motor road (take the latter if you're heading first to visit the **Ship 4** at Bowmanstead, a cosy traditional inn with an oak-beamed bar and real fire in winter – see alternative route on map) and then either keep the same bearing on the good track and later on grass and through two stiles to join the main road just south of the village, or follow the track as it later curves right and joins lake road close to the lake shore, when it's simply a left turn to walk up into Coniston village.

That's all the walking done so you can now enjoy your ale. However, a word of warning: Coniston in general is one of the most expensive sites in the Lakes and, whist I praise the beer quality, I wish I could be so enthusiastic about the prices.

Head first for the unmissable **Black Bull 2** right in the village centre by the bridge where we started. It occupies a photogenic location beneath the Yewdale Fells which offer a fine backdrop for the pub; it's the 'tap' for the nearby Coniston Brewery all of whose excellent beers are available here. Good food is also available, and you get a decent serving for your money.

If you can face the short sharp climb up the lane for the second time, the **Sun 3** offers the best range of ales in town. It's a handsome building with an atmospheric and spacious interior. Expect up to eight beers with a strong emphasis on local brews. Once again a wide menu is available if you choose to eat here.

PUB INFORMATION

1 Church House Inn
Torver, Coniston, LA21 8AZ
01539 441282
www.churchhouseinntorver.com
Opening Hours: 11-11 summer;
12-3, 5-11 winter

2 Black Bull
Coppermines Road, Coniston,
LA21 8HL
015394 41335
www.blackbullconiston.co.uk
Opening Hours: 11-11
(10.30 Sun)

3 Sun
Coniston, LA21 8HQ
015394 41248
www.thesunconiston.com
Opening Hours: 12-11.30

TRY ALSO:

4 Ship
Bowmanstead, Coniston,
LA21 8HB
015394 41224
www.shipinn.info
Opening Hours: 12-3, 6-11
(not Mon & Tue Nov-Mar)

▶ **LINK** By Blueworks bus X12 to Ulverston (walk 10), 14 miles. By summer bus 505 to Hawkshead (walk 12), 4 miles.

The Langdales from Elterwater

WALK INFORMATION

Start/Finish: Elterwater, by Britannia Inn

Access: Bus 516 Langdale bus from Ambleside stops in village centre

Distance: 5.9 miles (9km)

OS Map: OS Explorer OL7

Key attractions: Grasmere (and Dove cottage) 2 miles; Langdale Pikes

The pubs: Three Shires Inn, Little Langdale; Wainwrights Inn, Great Langdale; Britannia Inn, Elterwater. Try also: Talbot Bar (Skelwith Bridge Hotel), Skelwith Bridge

One of the most popular parts of Lakeland and for good reason: it's accessible, attractive and varied, with good footpaths at low and high levels. Great Langdale was once a lake floor but little Elter Water is all that is left of that body of water. The appealing village that took its name from the lake is the start and finish point for this pleasant circuit. The last part of the route crosses by a working quarry which is a reminder that Lakeland was once a thriving industrial area. Terrain is generally undemanding, and navigation should not pose too many problems. All three pubs on the walk offer a wide range of ales many from the vibrant Cumbrian brewing scene; and, together with the *Old Dungeon Ghyll* (walk 30), they jointly host an annual beer festival in May.

At High Park, looking west into the high fells of central Lakeland

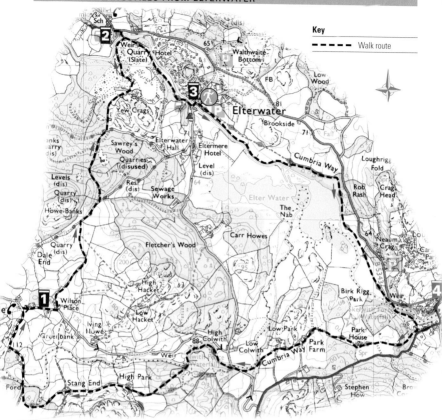

Key

- - - - Walk route

Start at the village green at Elterwater, by the Britannia Inn, which we save for later. The 516 Langdale bus from Ambleside will drop you right outside. Locate the bridleway opposite the pub and green signed for Skelwith Bridge. This runs along river on the near side and has recently been upgraded to accommodate cycles.

It's an easy path winding pleasantry between river and woodland with carpets of bluebells and wild garlic in spring, and when you reach the small lake there's a bench for an early stop to admire the scene – a typical Lakeland mixture of water, fell, and woodland. As you approach Skelwith Bridge the valley narrows and you'll reach a metal footbridge. Cross over this, unless you wish to sample the Thwaites beers at the **Talbot Bar 4** of the Skelwith Bridge Hotel in the village, in which case rejoin our route via the Cumbria Way across the main road bridge and double back along the southern shore of the river.

Follow the new cycle route as it climbs away from the river on the right-hand side of some houses. At the path junction where we meet the road from Skelwith Bridge, continue parallel to the road on the path marked 'Colwith Bridge'. This is the Cumbria Way, which continues to climb gently but steadily through the trees and out into a more open landscape, with views over to the fells including Wetherlam and the Langdale Pikes. Before long there's a steep descent to the river, and beyond this, you reach a quiet lane. Here, turn right following a sign for 'Colwith Force' and then leave the lane on the left in about 100 yards. Here, once through the gate, take the right-hand option, again marked 'Colwith Force'. The path climbs steadily and pleasantly through the woodland until just at a point where some steps climb higher you can detour a few yards to enjoy a good view of the waterfall, although there are also views further up on the main path when you get above it.

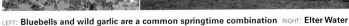

LEFT: **Bluebells and wild garlic are a common springtime combination** RIGHT: **Elter Water**

Up the steps and beyond, you emerge at the top of the woodland and follow the path right down to High Park Farm, a very good viewpoint. Below you lies the hamlet of Little Langdale in the valley. In a few yards leave the Cumbria Way and take the footpath on the right over a stile, keeping ahead on the small lane ignoring the footpath right, and forking right (signed 'Ambleside, Elter-water') at the junction at Stang End Farm beyond. Follow the very quiet unfenced lane, down the hill over the stream, then round to a bridge over the river, an idyllic spot. Then simply walk up the lane into Little Langdale, and at the 'main' road turn right and the **Three Shires Inn 1** is a few yards ahead on the left.

At the heart of this scattered community lying at the foot of the tortuous mountain road to Dud-don and Eskdale, the pub is well sited with fine views across the valley to the front. Unfortunately you have to be a resident to occupy the tempting benches in front of the building. To make up, the attractive modernised stone flagged bar, towards the rear and entered via the car park, offers four beers. Local brewers Coniston, Jennings and Hawkshead are among the most common offerings on the four handpumps on the bar with well-regarded new micro Ennerdale often in evidence too. Like the other pubs on this walk you'll get food at most hours; and like the others too the Three Shires is a participant in the annual Langdale beer festival held every May.

Continue down the road until you reach Wilson Place farm in about 200 yards, where there's a footpath running up through the farmyard and then onto the fell, climbing to join the wider Little Langdale to Elterwater bridleway at a gate. It's worth looking behind for a fine view of Wetherlam and the Old Man of Coniston. Turn right onto the bridleway, and immediately after passing through a gate take the left fork. This path climbs to a brow and a fabulous view opens out across to the Langdale Pikes. You'll quickly realise how high you still are, but the bridleway now descends very steeply to cross another lane by a house. Bear right and pick up the path shortly on the left and continue downhill, through some enormous quarry workings. It's not pretty but it's well signed, through the quarry and then down (with again

The Langdale Pikes dominate the scene on the descent to Wainwrights Inn

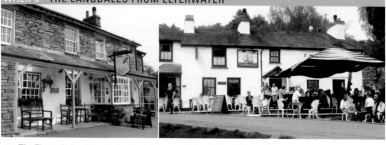

LEFT: **The Three Shires Inn, Little Langdale** RIGHT: **The Britannia Inn, Elterwater**

some stunning views of the Langdale Pikes) towards the river which you cross on a footbridge, having skirted a rocky knoll on the right.

This deposits you very conveniently right by the car park of **Wainwrights Inn** 2. It's a former gunpowder factory manager's house which took over from a now defunct pub, the White Lion, further up the road in the hamlet of Chapel Stile. It's internally attractive with a flagstone floor around the bar counter presided over by a large fireplace; separate drinking areas are arranged all round the bar servery. In summer, food is served all day until 9pm and service is good. The beer range won't disappoint either: three from the Banks's/Jennings stable complemented by up to four changing guests with the emphasis very much on Cumbrian brews. There's a separate dining area at the rear.

Retrace your steps over the river bridge, and follow the footpath immediately to the left this time which winds pleasantly up through the trees with the river noisily gushing through the rocky valley to your left. Emerge on the quarry road with an enormous cave immediately opposite. Walk down this road which is still in use so keep an eye open for lorries, and in no time you'll emerge right back where you started, in the centre of Elterwater, and this time the **Britannia Inn** 3 will be open and ready for you. A very well known and popular pub at the centre of this well-placed village, the Britannia will need no introduction to many. To their credit they have quite successfully married the sometimes competing demands of the walking drinker and the car-bound diner, and the right-hand room remains primarily for the former, although with my traditionalist hat on I still feel sore about the poshing up of the old little rear room which still exists but used to have its own bar counter and stone flagged floor. Having said that, the main public rooms retain much character with thick walls and oak-beamed low ceilings. Check the pub web site for details of accommodation, and the annual Champion of Champions beer festival in November. The six handpumps dispense regulars from Coniston, Jennings and Timothy Taylor alongside a wide range of changing guests; expect your beer to be in very good condition as evidenced by regular inclusion in the *Good Beer Guide*. In good weather there can be few better spots to enjoy a pint than the delightful green immediately outside with fine views unspoilt by the drone of any passing traffic.

PUB INFORMATION

1 Three Shires Inn
Little Langdale, Ambleside,
LA22 9NZ
015394 37215
www.threeshiresinn.co.uk
Opening Hours: 11-3; 8-10.30;
11-11 Fri & Sat; 12-3, 8-10.30 Sun
(winter); 12-10.30 Sun (summer)

2 Wainwrights Inn
The Langdale Estate, Great
Langdale, LA22 9JD
015394 38088
www.langdale.co.uk/dine/
wainwrights
Opening Hours: 12-11

3 Britannia Inn
Elterwater, Ambleside, LA22 9HP
015394 37210
www.britinn.net
Opening Hours: 11-11; 12-
10.30 Sun

TRY ALSO:

4 Talbot Bar
(Skelwith Bridge Hotel)
Skelwith Bridge, Ambleside,
LA22 9NJ
015394 32115
www.skelwithbridgehotel.co.uk
Opening Hours: 6-11; 12-2.30
Sat; 12-2, 6-10.30 Sun

LINK To Old Dungeon Ghyll (walk 30), via 516 Langdale bus, 4 miles. To Ambleside (walk 28) via 516 bus, 3 miles. To Coniston (walk 8) by 505 bus from Clappersgate, 3 miles.

An Ulverston town trail

WALK INFORMATION

Start: Coronation Hall, by Laurel & Hardy statue

Finish: Devonshire Arms

Access: Rail station 0.25 miles; buses X35 Kendal to Barrow or X12 from Coniston

Distance: 1.25 miles (2km); with detour 3.25 miles (5.25km)

OS Map: OS Explorer OL7

Key attractions: Laurel & Hardy museum and statue; Hoad Hill and monument; South Lakes Wild Animal Park, Dalton in Furness (4 miles); Furness Abbey (5 miles)

The pubs: Farmers Arms, Mill, Swan Inn, Stan Laurel Inn, Devonshire Arms, all Ulverston. Try also: Bay Horse Hotel, Ulverston

Thanks to its good rail and bus connections Ulverston is one of the best centres for exploring the South Lakes and Furness. It's big enough to feel like a proper town and has plenty of history, although it's perhaps best known for being the birthplace of Stan Laurel. Until recently Ulverston was home to the Hartleys brewery, taken over and closed by Robinson's of Stockport in 1991. The old brewery buildings watch over the town like a ghost and ill-feeling still rankles.

If you want to extend your walk the obvious option is Hoad Hill with its distinctive monument, but there's also a canalside stroll down to the harbour where there's a pub handily placed to break the journey. It's worth checking the opening times of the pubs before planning this walk: some don't open at lunchtimes and others have an afternoon closure…

Houses fronting the open square of the Gill

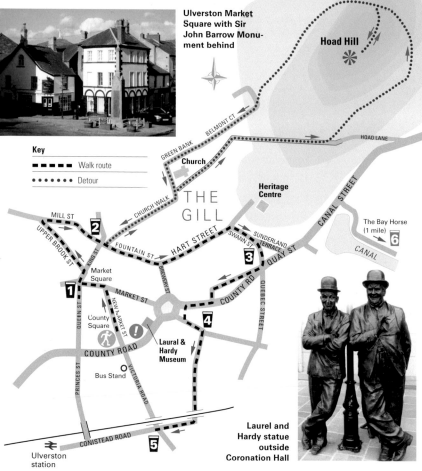

Ulverston Market Square with Sir John Barrow Monument behind

Hoad Hill

Key
- ▬ ▬ ▬ Walk route
- • • • • • Detour

GREEN BANK
BELMONT CT
HOAD LANE

Church

Heritage Centre

CANAL STREET

THE GILL

The Bay Horse (1 mile) **6**

CANAL

CHURCH WALK

MILL ST **2**

UPPER BROOK ST

KING ST

FOUNTAIN ST

HART STREET

SWANN ST

SUNDERLAND TERRACE

QUAY ST

3

BREWERY ST

Market Square

1

QUEEN ST

NEW MARKET ST

MARKET ST

COUNTY ROAD

PRINCES ST

VICTORIA ROAD

Bus Stand

County Square

(!)

COUNTY RD

QUEBEC STREET

4

Laural & Hardy Museum

CONISTEAD ROAD **5**

Ulverston station

Laurel and Hardy statue outside Coronation Hall

🚶 Start outside the handsome Coronation Hall in County Square at the centre of town, just a couple of minutes from the bus stands or a short walk from the station via Princes or Victoria Streets. The hall, which also houses the Tourist Information office, commemorates the accession of George V in 1911. Now largely traffic-free, the square is also home to several other notable civic buildings and of course a much more recent arrival, the rather good Laurel & Hardy statue. The bronze statue, created by artist Graham Ibbeson who also did the famous Eric Morecambe statue in Morecambe, was unveiled in April 2009. It was funded by the Sons of the Desert – the international appreciation society for Laurel and Hardy.

Walk up New Market Street and left, which brings you into the Market Square with its handsome war memorial. Now it's decision time: if you want to do the circuit around Hoad Hill, (see box) I'd recommend undertaking that before starting on the pubs – in which case, in consultation with your map, head up King Street into Church Walk, returning to the Farmers Arms and the Mill at the end of the circuit. Otherwise, the **Farmers Arms 1**, a handsome listed building, overlooks the Market Square and is a good place to start the day's drinking. In the front bar, six handpumps offer two Thwaites beers plus four rotating guests, and if the weather's good the pleasant patio outside fills up quickly. There's an attractive dining-orientated rear room.

Continue into King Street for about 50 yards and turn left into Upper Brook Street. This leads into a large open area known as the Gill. Once the site of Ulverston's old hiring fairs, it's now surrounded by attractive cottages, and usually littered with parked cars. You can walk round the Gill and spot the Town Beck at the head of the Gill, which is also the starting point for the Cumbria Way, a 70 mile traverse of the county to Carlisle. The circuit brings you back towards King Street via Mill Street and our next stop, the

Mill 2. This is a stylish conversion of the former town mill powered by the same now-culverted Town Beck, and the mill race and machinery can still be seen preserved in the building. It's all been done very nicely with a variety of seating areas arranged around the old machinery and an upstairs terrace/lounge/restaurant with live music on Mondays. Owned by the company that has developed the Lancaster brewery, expect to find their full range of four appealing beers and four guest beers sourced from across the country. There's also a good range of bottled beers particularly from Belgium and Germany. Food is served from a wide menu all day until 9pm, with a pizza menu on Sundays. The only bum note in this otherwise very good bar is the large mark-up encountered on half

Inside the Mill

pints, although in fairness prices for pints were very reasonable (especially in comparison to nearby tourist settlements!).

To continue the walk, head off along Fountain Street to the junction with Brewery Street and Hart Street. You'll see the remains of the old red brick brewery behind the street frontage, and if you detour a few yards down Brewery Street there's an information board in the car park, opposite the old brewery gates. Brewing here goes back to 1755. It became Hartleys in 1919, and for many years they vied with Jennings as the premier Cumbrian brewers. Sadly Hartleys was bought by Robinson's in 1982, and they in turn ended production, ending a proud record of 236 years of traditional brewing at this site. Some of the town's pub still have their Hartleys livery, so long has it taken Robinson's to upgrade them.

CIRCULAR WALK TO HOAD HILL AND SIR JOHN BARROW MONUMENT

At the top of King Street by the junction with Mill Street, the handsome Soutergate leads uphill out of town. Off to the right at 45-degrees, Church Walk leads up to the parish church of St Mary's. Through the churchyard a footpath (known as ladies walk) leads past a large standing stone of limestone and offers good views up to Hoad Hill and the Sir John Barrow Monument on your left. Fork left on the steadily but gently rising path, past a squirrel seat, avoiding the several very steep paths snaking up through the grass to save your breath. You can then approach the monument from the rear, enjoying extensive views over the town and across the bay

at the same time. The monument is a copy of the Eddystone Lighthouse and is open when the flag at the foot of the monument is flying. Sir John Barrow, born in Ulverston, was second secretary to the Admiralty and a founder member of the Royal Geographical Society. He died in 1848 and townsfolk had this landmark erected in his honour two years later.

There are several ways down off the hill – I recommend skirting the monument on the northern side and taking the clear path before then selecting the first left turn on another path which will bring you back via the church and Church Walk to arrive back at the top of King Street, close to the Mill.

The monument to Sir John Barrow on Hoad Hill

You'll need cheering up, so take Hart Street along the northern side of the old brewery, and follow it into Swan Street to the road junction at the far end where, sitting up above the road, lies the **Swan Inn 3** . This spacious double-fronted pub with three distinct drinking areas was the first tied house of the Hawkshead brewery, although they don't just offer their own fine beers here; you can expect to find Yates Bitter and around half a dozen changing guests from all round the country, making the Swan arguably the top destination in town for beer choice. There's no food however; and note that it doesn't open until 3.30 in the afternoon during the week.

This is the point at which you might wish to detour off piste and take the canal towpath down to the shore at the end of the mile-long Ulverston canal. The towpath is accessed from the main road a little further north – cross Swan Street and walk up the grassy bank to join Sunderland Terrace with its handsome curving aspect. At the far end it joins the busy 'A' road where you should cross with care and the towpath starts a little further on. At Canal Foot, overlooking the Leven estuary stands the **Bay Horse Hotel 6** with a varied selection of beers. Bus 60 returns you into town.

Back on the main trail outside the Swan, we're heading back into town a little, preferably on the quieter Newton Street, immediately right of the pub on exit, rather than along the unpleasant A590 beyond it. At the end of Newton Street join the main road left and continue along for a bit looking for an opportunity to cross safely. Sneak across the car showroom forecourt or go to the junction with The Ellers and bear left. This interesting street once had a couple of mills: High Ellers mill is across the road at the top of the street and is now a block of flats. Beyond it is the Lanternhouse, a striking contemporary arts venue transformed from a former national schools building. Of more interest to us perhaps is the establishment a

wee bit furthor down on the left, however. The **Stan Laurel Inn 4** isn't far behind the Swan in beer range, offering Thwaites Original and up to five changing guest beers (from local breweries in the main) in a friendly atmosphere. The place is festooned with Laurel & Hardy memorabilia, for Stan was born just round the corner in Argyll Street. This is also your last chance on the route to get some food, with good quality fare at reasonable prices every day except Mondays.

Take Chapel Street, almost opposite across The Ellers, and follow it down to the railway bridge. Under the railway and first left into Conishead Road, and you'll arrive at the **Devonshire Arms 5** at the next corner. This is a corner local pretty much off the visitors' radar, although it's close to the railway station, which makes it a handy finishing post if you're leaving by train. Another pub to have increased its beer range recently, you can expect a couple of ales from Lancaster and maybe three rotating guests, although it no longer opens at lunchtimes during the week nor offers food, so be warned!

Head back into town simply by walking under the railway and straight up Victoria Road past the bus stands. For the station continue along the rest of Conishead Road, and straight over.

PUB INFORMATION

1 Farmers Arms
Market Place, Ulverston, LA12 7AB
01229 584469
www.thefarmers-ulverston.co.uk
Opening Hours: 9.30am-11
(midnight Fri & Sat); 9.30am-
10.30 Sun

2 Mill
Town Mill, Mill Street, Ulverston,
LA12 7EB
01229 581384
www.mill-at-ulverston.co.uk
Opening Hours: 10-11.30pm
(midnight Fri & Sat; 11pm Sun)

3 Swan Inn
Swan Street, Ulverston, LA12 7JX
01229 869549
www.swaninnulverston.co.uk
Opening Hours: 3.30-11;
12-midnight Fri & Sat; 12-11 Sun

4 Stan Laurel Inn
31 The Ellers, Ulverston, LA12 0AB
01229 582814
www.thestanlaurel.co.uk
Opening Hours: 7-midnight
Mon; 12-2.30, 6-midnight Tue-
Sat; 12-midnight Sun

5 Devonshire Arms
1 Braddyll Terrace, Ulverston,
LA12 0DH
01229 582537
Opening Hours: 4-11; 3-mid-
night Fri; 12-midnight
Sat; 12-11 Sun

TRY ALSO:

6 Bay Horse Hotel
Canal Foot, Ulverston, LA12 9EL
01229 582537
www.thebayhorsehotel.co.uk
Opening Hours: 11-11; 12-
10.30 Sun

Lake Windermere from Sawrey

WALK INFORMATION

Start/ Finish: Ferry House car park (388954)

Access: Ferry from Bowness (for Windermere); summer bus 525 from Hawkshead

Distance: 6.8 miles (11km)

OS map: OS Explorer OL7

Key attractions: Lake shore path; Hill Top, Near Sawrey; Hawkshead village (2 miles); Graythwaite Hall & gardens (3 miles)

The pubs: Tower Bank Arms, Near Sawrey; Claife Crier Bar (Sawrey Hotel), Far Sawrey

A very satisfying circuit taking in a fine stretch of the western shore of England's largest lake, complemented by some quiet rural byways and bridleways. The two little villages of Near and Far Sawrey retain plenty of charm despite the main road bisecting both, and the Beatrix Potter industry at the former attracting huge numbers of visitors. Both the pubs on this walk are attractive buildings offering a good range of well-kept beers. If you're arriving from Windermere via the Bowness ferry, the start point is a couple of hundred yards up the road from the Ferry House, on the right-hand side of the road. Be aware that this is a relatively long route by the standards of this book: a much shorter option but without the pleasant lakeside walk would be to reverse the route from Ferry House and finish at the Tower Bank Inn, having arranged your return transport.

Lake Windermere in the early morning mist

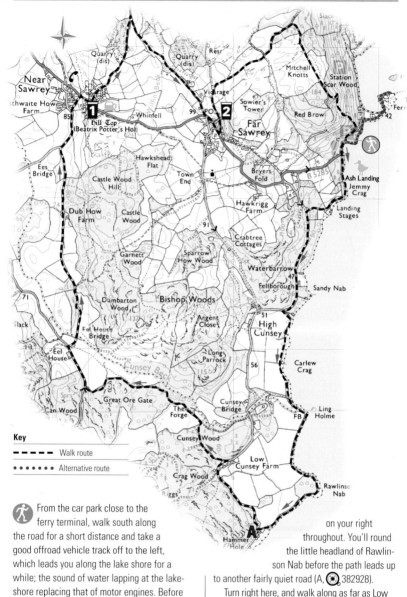

Key

- – – – – Walk route
- • • • • • Alternative route

From the car park close to the ferry terminal, walk south along the road for a short distance and take a good offroad vehicle track off to the left, which leads you along the lake shore for a while; the sound of water lapping at the lakeshore replacing that of motor engines. Before long however the track veers away from the lake, uphill, to join a minor lane.

Bear left here and walk along the lane for maybe half a mile until, as the road veers sharp right, find and take a signed footpath which leads back down to the shore. Be aware that there is no escape from this (albeit very pleasant) lakeside path for about a mile since there is private land on your right throughout. You'll round the little headland of Rawlinson Nab before the path leads up to another fairly quiet road (A, 382928).

Turn right here, and walk along as far as Low Cunsey Farm, about ¼ of a mile, then follow the bridlepath which leaves the road on your left, and soon bears right (don't go through the gate ahead) to join another bridlepath. Turn left and walk along a quiet little valley with a small stream, the Cunsey Beck, a few yards away on your right. Improbable as it now seems there was once an ironworks here marked on the map as 'The Forge'

A glimpse of Lake Windermere through the trees from Mitchell Knotts

CLAIFE STATION & THE PICTURESQUE MOVEMENT

Near the end of the walk you'll pass the ruins of Claife Station. This viewing station is a fragment of an interesting piece of history. Thomas West published the first Lake District guidebook in 1778, at a time when the so-called Picturesque Movement was gaining ground. The Picturesque Movement, a reaction to the ordered, smooth rolling landscapes of the likes of Capabilty Brown, contended that landscapes should only be viewed from certain points, at their most appealing. These viewpoints became the fashionable places for tourists and artists to visit, and around Lake Windermere alone there are seven recorded sites, including Claife. Here as at other viewing stations, visitors could turn their backs to the landscape, hold up a tinted mirror known as a Claude Glass (named after the paintings of Claude Lorraine) and look at the framed and transformed view. The mirror would make the scene easier to draw and record. In addition, each of the windows within the drawing room had different coloured glass, and a different aspect, enabling seasonal variations to be accentuated. For instance, yellow represented summer, orange was for autumn, light green for spring, and light blue for winter. There was also a dark blue tint for moonlight and lilac to suggest a thunderstorm.

Claife station was built in the last decade of the eighteenth century, and reached the height of its popularity before the mid point of the next, by which time the Picturesque Movement was in decline. Today it looks pretty sorry for itself but maybe it will eventually be restored.

and associated with a furnace nearby on the lake shore. Remains of the wheelpit and some associated buildings, once in the control of the large Backbarrow company (see walk 7) survive in the undergrowth.

This now very green and pleasant stretch brings you out onto a busier road which, having turned right, you follow (keeping well in and facing the traffic) for a short way until a much smaller lane leads off to the right by Eel House and crosses the Cunsey Beck. From here it's simply a mile's pleasant walk past Dub How to Near Sawrey, with views of Esthwaite Water and, further afield, the Langdale Pikes, in the later stages. As you near the village, fork right at the choice of lanes and then at the T-junction it's right

Near Sawrey

LEFT: **Imaginative use of old stables in the Claife Crier** RIGHT: **Tower Bank Arms, Near Sawrey**

again past Beatrix Potter's Hill Top (probably mobbed with Japanese tourists who for some reason find her irresistable) and just beyond, the rather attractive **Tower Bank Arms 1**. This little pub is owned by the National Trust and despite some modernisation retains a simple, unpretentious interior with stone floor and comfortable chairs. You'll be able to choose from up to five beers: a couple from Hawkshead with guests coming from Cumbrian brewers. Food is served lunchtimes and evenings.

Leaving the pub look for the lane which runs off almost opposite and, taking this, climb past some pretty cottages, beyond which the road becomes a offroad vehicle track and bridleway, with pleasant rural views opening out across the village to the wooded hills beyond. After a few minutes another equally wide track joins from the right. Take this by turning sharply back to the right and walk down directly into Far Sawrey in a few more minutes. Bear left on the main road and in a couple of moments you arrive at the **Claife Crier Bar 2** attached to the Sawrey Hotel. Like the Tower Bank this is an attractive whitewashed old building with plenty of character. Named for a local ghost, it's a former stable block and there's no mistaking this since some of the drinking area occupies the old stalls. You can expect up to six beers: Theakston Best Bitter, Jennings Cumberland and Sneck Lifter, alongside three from Hawkshead Brewery.

Turn left when leaving the pub and take the signed bridleway just beyond the car park which climbs back sharply on the left and rises gently at first and then more steeply onto the open hillside above the village. Once again good views open out across this unspoilt part of the Lake District.

Once you get to the top of the path and cross over a right of way coming in from the left, continue on the main path towards the woodland, which becomes an attractive tree-lined route with a wall on either side.

It's easy to miss the footpath down to the ferry which leads off to the right through a gate. It's just before you reach a gate on the main bridleway. The path runs into the woods and this stretch is arguably the highlight of the walk: there are great views from the top of the steep bank down to the lake with its marinas, with Bowness on the far shore and fells beyond. You're at quite a height above the lake. At a second post the path then descends steeply through the woods (care needed) towards the shore. Near the foot of the hill we come across the remains of Claife Station (see box). Just below the station the footpath divides. If you're heading down to the ferry bear left (signed) otherwise take the steps signed 'Ash landing and Hill Top' which leads out to the car park by the road where we began.

PUB INFORMATION

1 Tower Bank Arms
Near Sawrey, Ambleside,
LA22 0LF
015394 36334
www.towerbankarms.co.uk
Opening Hours: 11-11 (closed 2.30-5.30 Mon-Fri winter); 12-10.30 Sun

2 Claife Crier Bar
(Sawrey Hotel)
Far Sawrey, Ambleside, LA22 0LQ
015394 43425
www.sawrey-hotel.co.uk
Opening Hours: 11-11, 12-10.30 Sun

▶ LINK Hawkshead (walk 12) via summer bus 525, 2 miles.

Circuit of Latterbarrow from Hawkshead

WALK INFORMATION

Start/Finish: Hawkshead village

Access: In summer, bus 505 Windermere/Ambleside to Coniston via Hawkshead. Bus 525 from Sawrey Ferry House (ferry from Bowness/ Windermere). Check times carefully

Distance: 3.4 miles (5.4km)

OS map: OS Explorer OL7

Key attractions: Hawkshead village and old grammar school; Beatrix Potter's house (2 miles)

The pubs: King's Arms, Hawkshead. Try also: Drunken Duck, Barngates

One of the few routes in this book which can claim to visit a fell top, albeit a pretty low one whose summit height is only 803 feet (244 metres). Despite the lack of altitude the fell is well loved for its fine views, and is another summit praised by Wainwright despite its lowly elevation. The summit cairn is impressive, and can be seen from Hawkshead village – the start and finish of the route. The climb to the felltop is easy to follow, and taken in the recommended direction not steep, the easy half-day saunter leaving you time to explore the area further. Drinkers can enjoy the agreeable setting of the King's Head where you'll be able to drink beers from Hawkshead's eponymous brewery, and all three of the village's other pubs serve real ale.

Lake Windermere from Latterbarrow

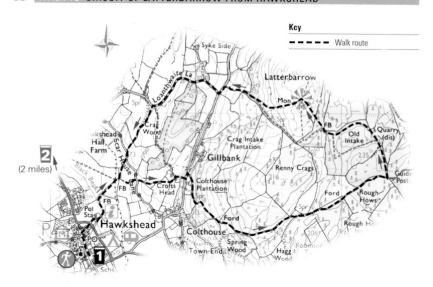

Key

– – – – – Walk route

Leave Hawkshead by the *Red Lion* pub and look for the footpath sign immediately north of the building which leads down past some houses and brings you out at the bypass road. Cross straight over and continue – the path bears slightly to the right – until you reach a gate across a stream. Bear left here and follow the riverside path for a few yards before leaving it on another path on a bearing of about 45-degrees,

A cobbled street in old Hawkshead

which leads to a field gate. Continue in the same direction to a second gate where there is a choice of routes. Take the right-hand option signed 'Colthouse'. In no time this brings you to a tiny lane (Scar House Lane on the map) which you cross over: a short steep climb up the bank and you should find another stile and once over this, a series of well-marked stiles and gates brings you to another tiny tarred lane by an attractive cottage. Bear right and up to the minor road ahead. The tiny hamlet of Colthouse with some unspoilt cottages is a short stroll along on the right if you like Lakeland buildings. The Quakers were once influential in this area and interestingly there is a 17th-century Friends' Meeting House with an old burial ground in Colthouse. Otherwise turn left, but only as far as the entrance to Gillthwaite, a few yards on the right – here a signed bridleway bears sharply back to the right with a gate through the deer fence. Now it's simply a matter of following this good bridleway for about a mile, climbing steadily through open woodland. Eventually, as you reach the summit of the bridleway, you'll see the prominent summit cairn of Latterbarrow quite close by on your left. You actually start to descend a wee bit before reaching a signpost offering you a route on the left towards Latterbarrow. The cairn is still visible, not much higher than you are. The downside is that the route to reach it follows a convoluted

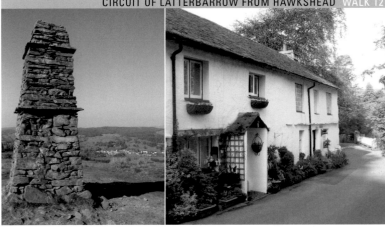

LEFT: **The summit cairn on Latterbarrow** RIGHT: **Cottages in Colthouse**

course, as it meanders around a newly clear-felled and fenced area and then zig zags rather drunkenly (but always clearly on the ground). The fell has been spared the covering of trees which cloak a good deal of the uplands between Lake Windermere and Hawkshead's lake, Esthwaite Water, and you will be able to appreciate the fine views *en route* to the summit.

God willing you will reach the summit before long, where you can enjoy wide views especially over the northern half of the panorama. Fell tops include the Old Man group; Bowfell & Crinkle Crags; the Langdale Pikes, Loughrigg Fell (the lower fell) and the Helvellyn range — and if you walk across thirty yards, you'll get an excellent view of Lake Windermere. Leaving, the path you

Colthouse

King's Arms, Hawkshead

want is the one due west – if you're not in mist simply head off in the direction of Hawkshead village below, about 90-degrees from the direction from which you arrived. It's a steep but well-defined path which quickly returns you to the minor road you left earlier. Bear left a few yards and then right down another road (Loanthwaite Lane) which meanders pleasantly through the trees until you arrive at two footpaths, both signed, in quick succession on your left. Take the second one ('Hawkshead') which offers open views to your right as it leads gently downhill to Scar House Lane, where the path continues in the same direction a few yards down. This section deposits you at the double-finger post you met early on in the walk when you turned right for Colthouse. This time, retrace your steps through the fields and across the river before walking back up into the village.

Hawkshead is a compact and charming settlement: if it has a fault it's that it does get loved to death by the trippers, and you're one too so it's hard to complain. The **King's Arms** 1 is probably the best bet for ale drinkers, and it's enviably sited right in the middle of the small square in the village centre. The bar is spacious and characterful, although you might wish to sit outside in good weather and enjoy the pleasant square which isn't disturbed by through traffic. There's a separate dining room if you want to be more formal, whilst the hotel offers serviced and self catering accommodation. Expect up to four well-kept beers on offer including at least one from Coniston, Hawkshead and Black Sheep. The Hawkshead Brewery is ironically no longer situated in the village of the same name – expansion meant that they had to relocate to Staveley (see walk 16) in 2006.

If you've got time you may wish to explore the attractive old streets of Hawkshead, one of the National Park's most attractive villages, and where William Wordsworth was schooled, or if you're game for more walking you can link with other nearby routes. If you have access to your own transport or can call a cab, you might consider visiting the **Drunken Duck** 2 at Barngates, a couple of miles north. This is a pub which brews its own ales, although it's well upmarket with prices to match and I have never felt too comfortable with the ambience.

PUB INFORMATION

1 King's Arms
The Square, Hawkshead,
LA22 0NZ
015394 36372
www.kingsarmshawkshead.co.uk
Opening Hours: 11-midnight

TRY ALSO:

2 Drunken Duck
Barngates, Ambleside, LA22 0NG
015394 36347
www.drunkenduckinn.co.uk
Opening Hours: 11-midnight

LINK To walk 11, via B 5285 road, 2 miles (summer bus 525). Summer bus 505 to Coniston (walk 8), 3½ miles.

Westmorland Group – the South East

A fine old house in Troutbeck village

Kirkby Lonsdale & the River Lune

WALK INFORMATION

Start/Finish: Market Square, Kirkby Lonsdale

Access: 'Lune villager' bus 81A/B from Lancaster; 567 from Kendal

Distance: 5.5 miles (9km)

OS map: OS Explorer OL2

Key attractions: Historic market town of Kirkby Lonsdale; Devil's Bridge; Ingleton attractions including waterfalls walk (7 miles)

The pubs: Orange Tree, Sun, Plato's, all Kirkby Lonsdale. Try also: Avanti, Kirkby Lonsdale

A leisurely circuit starting and finishing at this attractive market town which feels shorter than it is on account of the easy terrain. The first half is a rural stroll to the small village of Whittington, the return follows the riverside path via the handsome Devil's Bridge before curving along the river banks under the town and climbing up to the churchyard, with several decent watering holes a mere stone's throw away. Kirkby Lonsdale was one of the few towns in the region mentioned in the Domesday Book. Today it boats an appealing range of handsome 18th-century buildings and more modest cottages, as well as some very modern bars reflecting the upwardly mobile aspirations of the place as a whole – the irredeemably old-fashioned might want to settle for the traditional pubbiness of the Orange Tree. Kirkby Lonsdale is also a gateway to the Yorkshire Dales National Park, indeed the iconic flat topped Ingleborough Hill is visible early on in the walk.

Devil's Bridge at Kirkby Lonsdale

The solid church tower at Whittington

Key

– – – – Walk route

• • • • • • • Detour

Start the walk from the Market Square by the Market Cross: take the main street by turning left out of the Market Square and walk down to the A65 road. Carefully cross into the road almost opposite and continue along here for some 200 yards looking out for a footpath up a bank off on the right which is not very obvious but is right opposite a far more visible path on the left, near the end of the houses.

Climb straightaway up a steep bank which immediately gives you views across to the distinctive flat topped Ingleborough Hill behind you. Keep to the left-hand wall, passing through the bank of trees beyond it and continue through a series of stiles ignoring unmarked stiles and paths left, as far as you can go until you get to the white house with its conservatory. Go through the metal gate on your left and across a paddock with, 50 yards ahead, a finger post by a white cottage (Wood End). Once through here bear left on the bridleway marked 'Sellet Mill'. It's a pleasant shady path with trees on both sides although at times you'll

be sharing the route with a stream bed and the going underfoot is very stony.

Reaching the small hamlet of Sellet turn right on a footpath over a curious stile to keep on the right-hand side of the hedge (not through the farmyard below). Now look for a waymark on the first gate you get to beyond the buildings, leading across a small paddock to another gate to a few yards down (there may be a sign warning you of bulls in this field but if you can't see them you'll get across the small paddock before they could appear!). Once through this lower gate turn right and follow the line of telegraph poles along the lower end of the field with Sellet Hill on your left. Just before the telegraph wires disappear over the fence on your right look out for a stile crossing into the right-hand field below a house (Sellet Hall). Follow up and round the house to exit onto the lane by a junction.

Here, bear left onto a small lane (signed Whittington), and follow this for about half a mile. You shouldn't be bothered with much traffic. At the junction, turn left and enter the village of Whittington, passing the handsome and impressive church on your right, with a millennium mosaic at the entrance. At the road junction the route bears left but you have the option of a short detour right to the *Dragon's Head*, about 250 yards down just beyond the village hall. It's a stone pub offering a couple of beers but the opening hours, especially at lunchtime when you're likely to be here, seem erratic, and I can't vouch for the beer quality, so for these reasons it's not 'officially' recommended!

In either case, picking up from the road junction, bear left (or right, coming from the Dragon's Head), and look out for a signpost pointing off right after a few yards. Take this path away from the road across a rough lane and through the double gates (which I found tied, so you may need to climb them). Continue in the same direction through a gateway and then directly ahead on a path which becomes grassy and leads directly down to the river (A, ⊙ 610762). Here take the stile left to join the riverside path, a simple and pleasant stroll along the river to reach the main road back in about 20 minutes. Expect plenty of birdlife and activity along the river.

Just beyond the busy main road is the now-bypassed Devil's Bridge (see box). These days it's a popular gathering ground for bikers.

From the Devils Bridge it's an easy half a mile back into the town; simply follow the river path as far as an attractive building set back from the river bank at Mill Ayre, where there is an information plaque, and by an adjacent far uglier building a

Kirkby Lonsdale

THE DEVIL'S BRIDGE

This well-known structure is a very handsome beast. The legend associated with the bridge – that it was built by the devil – is a variation of one which crops up in other places. It is said that many years ago, before there was a bridge over the river here, an old woman lived on the banks of the Lune and kept a few animals. One night her cow strayed across to the other side of the river and wouldn't return. Suddenly the Devil appeared and promised to build a bridge by morning in exchange for a soul – the first to cross the bridge – thinking that it would be the woman herself. By morning the bridge was complete and the old woman agreed to fulfil her part of the bargain. She delved into her bag and threw a bun across the bridge, whereupon her small dog ran over to retrieve it. The devil, in a fit of rage at being outfoxed, screamed in anger and vanished in a cloud of burning brimstone.

---

sloping lane runs straight up into the town. An attractive alternative is to continue for a short distance along the riverside before reaching a flight of steps (and be warned there are over 80 of them!) at the top of which you'll exit into the northern edge of the churchyard, close to the bluff which overlooks the river valley and has become known as 'Ruskin's view'. In fact the worthy social theorist came across the view secondhand, as it were, since he was inspired to exclaim after seeing a painting of the scene by Turner: "I do not know in all my own country, still less in France or Italy, a place more naturally divine".

If you go up the steep Mill Brow into town aim for the churchyard of St Mary's on

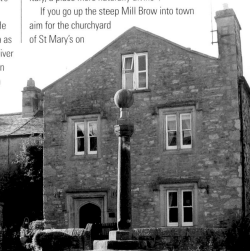

LEFT: **The Orange Tree features local beers** RIGHT: **The Dragon's Head at Whittington**

the right (take the alleyway opposite Horsemarket or Church Street, the narrow lane by the Sun Hotel) – otherwise from the top of the steps and Ruskin's View you're practically at the north-west corner of the churchyard. The church of St Mary's is itself worth a look: the oldest parts are three Norman columns in the nave, two carved with diamond motifs.

From the churchyard exit on the southern side into Fairbank, the B6254, and just a few doors along on the street is the **Orange Tree** ◼1. Formerly the Fleece Inn, this handsome town pub is probably the best bet in town for interesting ales. It has been opened out but retains some secluded corners and attractive features, foremost among them being the lovely range and fireplace. There's an atmospheric restaurant at the rear of the pub. Up to five ales are available on handpump, and among these expect at least a couple from the local Kirkby Lonsdale Brewery, for which the Orange Tree is the premier outlet. Their beers are named after local connections, and pumpclips remind you about the legendary bridge.

Returning to the town centre via the churchyard, you can't fail to miss the **Sun** ◼2 occupying a prime location on quiet Church Street. The Sun retains a very attractive historic façade, particularly on the Market Street frontage; but the place has followed the rest of the town upmarket, and indeed it's more of an eatery these days. Don't let this put you off a visit though: the attractive bar area boasts

some oak floorboards and offers up to four ales including Timothy Taylor Landlord and probably one from Jennings and Hawkshead.

Leaving the Sun, turn left into Market Street, and follow down to the junction with Mill Brow and Main Street. Here on the left is Kirkby Lonsdale's latest addition on the real-ale scene, **Plato's** ◼3. It's again an upmarket brasserie cum restaurant cum 'boutique hotel' – the stylish bar with its quality fittings has a very modern ambience – but it's worth a visit for the three cask beers, usually Black Sheep and at the time of writing, one from Kirkby Lonsdale and Tirril.

If you're game for another bar, you could try **Avanti** ◼4 on Main Street a stone's throw from Plato's: it's yet another ultra-modern place set back down an alleyway. There's a dining balcony specialising in pizzas, or you can remain downstairs and sample the Black Sheep Bitter.

The Market Place, where you began the walk, is a hundred yards down to the left when you leave Avanti.

PUB INFORMATION

◼1 **Orange Tree**
9 Fairbank, Kirkby Lonsdale,
LA6 2BD
01524 271716
www.theorangetreehotel.co.uk
Opening Hours: 12-11 (midnight Fri & Sat)

◼2 **Sun**
Market Street, Kirkby Lonsdale,
LA6 2AU
015242 71965
www.sun-inn.info
Opening Hours: 11-11

◼3 **Plato's**
2 Mill Brow, Kirkby Lonsdale,
LA6 2AT
015242 74180
www.platoskirkbylonsdale.co.uk
Opening Hours: 8-midnight
(11 Sun)

TRY ALSO:

◼4 **Avanti**
57 Main Street, Kirkby Lonsdale,
LA6 2AH
015242 73500
www.baravanti.com
Opening Hours: 11-11; 12-10.30 Sun

Ambleside to Troutbeck via Skelghyll Wood & Jenkin Crag

WALK INFORMATION

Start: Waterhead, Ambleside (⊙ 377032)

Finish: Troutbeck (optional return to Ambleside)

Access: Bus 554/555/556 runs from Kendal and Windemere to Keswick, via Ambleside

Distance: 2.8 miles (4.6km) to Troutbeck; 5.7 miles (9km) for circuit returning via Wansfell Pike

OS map: OS Explorer OL7

Key attractions: Skelgyll Wood; Jenkin Crag (viewpoint); Town End, Troutbeck; Brockhole visitor centre (2 miles)

The pubs: Mortal Man, Troutbeck

Ambleside with all its traffic may not be a particularly pretty place, but there's no denying it's a great spot from which to enjoy some top quality walks. This is one of them. It quickly climbs out of town and offers you excellent views across Windermere, England's largest lake. Troutbeck is arguably the most unspoilt village in the national park with many wonderful vernacular houses. And if you opt to return to Ambleside over Wansfell Pike, you'll be rewarded with views out of all proportion to the fairly modest height of the fell. Without this option it's a linear walk with no public transport at the far end; accordingly plan ahead with a cab or be prepared for an additional couple of miles' walk along the lane back to Troutbeck Bridge. The first half mile has a pretty steep gradient then it's easy, unless you're traversing Wansfell Pike which is over 1,500 feet high.

Looking across Windermere from near Jenkin Crag

Key

– – – – Walk route

• • • • • • Optional return

High Skelghyll farm

Start this walk at Waterhead, almost a mile to the south of the centre of Ambleside, by the junction of the two main roads and the Waterhead Hotel. Look for the footpath which leaves the main road on the left (heading east), almost opposite the junction. Be warned that the first section is by far the steepest of the whole walk! You climb up between the buildings and follow the path around, first to the right and then through a stile and up across a field which leads you onto the lower parts of Skelghyll Wood. The path still climbs steeply so take your time. In spring the whole floor is carpeted with a sea of bluebells and wild garlic.

Continue uphill steadily and, crossing a minor footpath, about 20 yards beyond you reach the main bridleway. Join this, turning right, and continue uphill swinging right over the beck and climbing further until eventually the path levels out (phew!). Resist the temptation to rest here since in a further hundred yards or so a gap in the wall on the right and a National Trust sign directs you to Jenkin Crag which is an excellent viewpoint with delightful views out across Lake Windermere. It's well worth the short stroll across, and you can enjoy a well-earned rest.

The woodland itself is really charming with oak dominating the mixture of native species. Birdsong is prevalent. Once you leave the woodland the landscape opens out into a mixture of

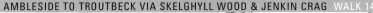

LEFT: **View from Wansfell Pike** RIGHT: **Town End, Troutbeck**

fell pasture with drystone walls. Pass High Skelghyll farm, and keep on the bridleway (blue arrow) by the beck just beyond the farm by turning left to stay on the wide track with good views out across the lake.

After another half a mile or so a well-placed seat by a junction of paths is a good spot to open your flask and enjoy the view. From here it's about another half a mile before the path joins the road by the Post Office in the village of Troutbeck. Much of this long straggling village is a real treat with numerous lovely old buildings strung out along the quiet road. One of the best is the National Trust's Town End, which you can visit by walking back down the road to the right for about ¼ of a mile.

To continue, bear left past the Post Office and in about 200 yards, by a double-fronted white cottage, take the bridleway down to the right and bear left by High Fold guest house. This is a pleasant walled bridleway which leads you into the valley towards the church which interestingly is some distance from the village. Cross the stream by a gate – you'll see the church a few yards after you start rising beyond the beck.

A fine old house in Troutbeck village

The path itself bears left about 50 yards before the church, opposite the top corner of the churchyard. Take the left of two signed paths. The next section is a charming stroll along a grassy terrace above the small stream, probably with plenty of fluffy sheep to add colour. You'll see by now the **Mortal Man**  in your sights ahead. To reach it most easily just keep as close to straight ahead as you can, and follow the lane (tarred in its later stages) as it curves up to bring you to the front door of the hotel. Dating back to 1689, this prominent hotel has recently been refurbished, and by the evidence, the new owners are getting this fine old building back to where it should be after a difficult period under the previous management. The comfortable but not overly tarty bar offers a good range of real ales. If the weather's good you can drink in the beer garden, which surely has some of the finest views of any Lakeland pub. The Mortal Man's unusual name derives from a sign painted for an erstwhile landlady at the pub. The old sign which I remember had deteriorated badly and, to their credit, the new owners have commissioned a replacement which comes complete with the little ditty about the good woman's beer. The place comes with food and accommodation, and with luck will once again become a destination of class in the national park, at a safe distance from the fleshpots of Ambleside.

Your choices once you leave the Mortal Man are really threefold. It's about a 2 mile walk back down past Town End (just follow the lane above the Mortal Man back down the valley) to the main road at Troutbeck

Bridge where you can pick up a bus on the A591. If you are in a group the more attractive option would be to have booked a cab to return you into Ambleside. If you're part of the intrepid minority and can face the climb after your ale, the high level return walk over Wansfell Pike offers some delightful views if the weather is favourable. Be warned that it is hardly a stroll with a climb to almost 1,600 feet, and unless you're an experienced hillwalker my advice would be to consult a fell walking guide, perhaps one of Mr Wainwright's, before attempting the route. The start of the walk is easy to find however – simply start the walk back down the road above the Mortal Man for less than 200 yards and you reach the signed route on the right almost opposite another path on the left. The descent from the summit is quite steep in places but you'll have plenty of beer choice to look forward to on your return to Ambleside – consult walk 28 for advice.

> **LINK** Walk 28 starts in Grasmere, a short bus ride (555) from Ambleside – or reverse the route from Ambleside itself.

PUB INFORMATION

1 Mortal Man
Troutbeck, LA23 1PL
015394 33193
www.themortalman.co.uk
Opening Hours: 11-12;
12-11 Sun

Scout Crag & Sizergh from Kendal

WALK INFORMATION

Start: Highgate, Kendal, junction of Allhallows Road

Finish: Strickland Arms (optional return to Kendal)

Access: Rail to Kendal from Windermere, Oxenholme and Lancaster. Bus 555 Lancaster to Keswick, X35 from Barrow and Furness, 567 from Kirkby Lonsdale; other local services

Distance: To the Strickland Arms: 6.4 miles (10.2km); complete circuit: 11 miles (17.2km)

OS map: OS Explorer OL7

Key attractions: Serpentine Woods; limestone scars and pavements of Scout Crag; Sizergh Castle; Low Sizergh Barn and tearoom; Kendal

The pubs: Strickland Arms, Great Strickland

The bold limestone escarpment running north-south on the western side of Kendal is a real surprise for walkers more used to the high fells of the central Lakes: even the late great Mr Wainwright waxed lyrical about the delights of the route out of Kendal and up to the remarkably bold drop of the limestone crag where it plunges into the wide Lyth valley. The exit from Kendal through the historic Serpentine Woods provides a quick and attractive entry onto the pleasant limestone slopes above the town. Fittingly for a book of pub walks the route culminates in a visit to a fine hostelry, set close to the National Trust's Sizergh Castle, where you can enjoy a range of ales and toast a former owner of the estate who, legend has it, built the pub to save his having to travel too far to take his pleasure.

Admiring the fine view from Scout Scar

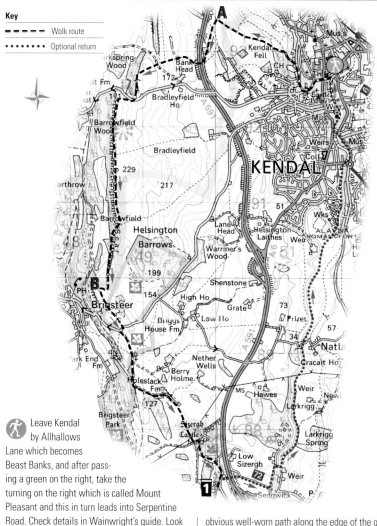

Key
- – – – – Walk route
•••••••• Optional return

Leave Kendal
by Allhallows
Lane which becomes
Beast Banks, and after passing a green on the right, take the
turning on the right which is called Mount
Pleasant and this in turn leads into Serpentine
Road. Check details in Wainwright's guide. Look
out for the stone gate pillars leading discreetly
into Serpentine Woods on the left just beyond the
railings ahead of you.

There are several paths here, so keep right,
close to the lower fence and within sight of the
road below you. When you emerge onto a wider
path there's a fork ahead of you. Take the upper
path here on the left just after a very steep section. Beyond this you emerge into the open and
there's a thoughtfully placed seat where you can
enjoy a panoramic view over Kendal and across
to the fells beyond. Nearby there's a waymark
sign with a number six on it. Now follow the fairly

obvious well-worn path along the edge of the golf
course on the left.

Soon the path is climbing steeply again through
an area of hawthorn and other native species.
The path levels out by couple of golf greens; keep
the same broad direction onto a grassy track
ahead of you. You'll join a wide grassy path (with
waymarks signed) a few yards across to your
right. Leave the golf course by a stone stile, and
once through a second stile, you'll see ahead of
you, with the noise of the bypass by now very
apparent, a pair of ladder stiles at the far end of
the next field. At this point (A, ⊕ 500934) turn
sharp left and follow the wall downhill curving

Sizergh Castle

left again at the bottom to make for a break in two lines of trees ahead of you. The right of way on the ground is unclear here, but drop down the little bank by a sycamore tree and a weird shaped trunk of another dying tree, and down to the farm buildings below you. A concrete slope which you follow down leads into the small hamlet here; pass through the gate and follow the tarred road as it bears around to the left with the noise of the bypass route very close by on your right. Look for a footpath sign leading into the trees towards the road in about a hundred yards, and take this through the woods to emerge on the roadside.

Cross this dual carriageway with great care, maybe moving a little to your left to improve the sightlines; once across the road you'll see the footpath carrying on through the wall by a telegraph post. Follow this up the bank and, joining a wall, use this as a handrail to climb the hill through a couple of stiles and directly up onto the open hillside of Cunswick Fell, making for an isolated finger board ahead of you. This directs

you left towards the mast – simply then follow the footpath up across a bridleway into a small copse right below the big mast. The path snakes through the trees, emerging into a car park by the road. Here a small path along the road avoids a 200 yard roadside walk, bringing you back to road by a second car park. Cross the road and take the signed footpath for Scout Crag.

Now follow the wide track which offers you a tremendous view across to the fells. You can switch onto autopilot for the next stretch as you walk along the crest of Scout Crag for well over a mile with wonderful views out to the west across to the Scafell group and the Langdale Pikes, even

The Scout Crag escarpment

LEFT: **The handsome Strickland Arms** RIGHT: **Smart but classy interior of the Strickland Arms**

right down to the estuary by Arnside and Silverdale. Pass the curious summit shelter and continue along at more or less a steady height, keeping to the right of a wall ahead of you and ignoring the steep footpath on your right down to Barrowfield.

Eventually a spur of land projects out to the right (B, ⊙ 484898) and you'll arrive at a kissing gate through another wall. Now for the first time a view opens up towards the south; take the central of three grassy tracks, heading more or less for the chapel which you can see about a mile ahead of you. This path runs down to a gate leading you onto a minor road. Turn right here and after 50 yards turn left onto the unfenced road leading down to the chapel. This is now part of the National Trust's Sizergh estate. Unusually for the Lake District the ground immediately below you on the right resembles the Fens rather than uplands: very flat and crossed by a series of drainage channels. The Leven estuary is beyond, and if the light's good you'll be able to make out the railway viaduct as the coastal line crosses the sands.

Pass the chapel, pausing briefly perhaps to inspect the directional indicators on the roadside, and continue ahead onto the signed footpath to Sizergh which takes you pleasantly and gently downhill, past the National Trust's interesting Holeslack farmhouse with its curved chimneys. Passing through a gate take the right-hand of two footpath options, this plunges seductively downhill into a shady narrow tree-lined pathway and is a delightful short stretch. All too soon, by an ugly farm building, bear right onto a wide stony track leading you down towards Sizergh Castle. Go through a gate and under the electricity pylons, and down to the entrance to the Castle and grounds.

By the National Trust ticket office and facing the entrance to the estate office and house, the quickest way to the pub is to take the wide estate drive to the right which you follow downhill and turning right at the bottom this brings you right out to your quarry, the **Strickland Arms** 1, for a well-deserved pint. After a period of closure this large estate pub has been very tastefully refurbished in a style well suited to the gravitas of the building. The bar room with its lovely fireplace and stone floor is light and airy, and a fine location to enjoy the range of interesting ales: expect up to five beers with the regulars being one from Thwaites and something from the Cumbrian Legendary Ales brewery, the new name for the Kirkstile Inn's Loweswater set-up. You can dine well here (and there's a separate room more given over to eating) both at lunchtimes until 2pm and in the evenings until 9pm (all day Sunday).

It's not much more than a five minute walk down to the main road for the frequent Kendal bus service (ask in the pub if unsure). Conversely, walkers wishing to continue on foot back to Kendal via the riverside valley path should bear left then right out of the pub and under the dual carriageway down Nannypie Lane to the river, picking up a footbridge to the right-hand bank a little way north. Consult your map...

If you want to spend longer exploring the area or the castle, Low Sizergh barn, with its recommended tearoom, is just to the north of the pub: head back towards the castle and follow the signs.

PUB INFORMATION

1 Strickland Arms
Great Strickland, CA10 3DF
01931 712238
www.thestricklandarms.co.uk
Opening Hours: 12-2.30 (not Mon & Tue), 5-11; 12-12 Sat; 12-10.30 Sun

A Staveley circuit via the Kentmere Valley & Ings

WALK INFORMATION

Start/Finish: Ings

Access: Buses from Kendal and Windemere to Ings, trains to Staveley

Distance: 8.7 miles (14km)

OS map: OS Explorer OL7

Key attractions: Kentmere Valley; Windermere & Bowness (3 miles); Kendal (4 miles)

The pubs: Eagle & Child, Beer Hall, both Staveley; Watermill Inn, Ings

Outside of the main tourist areas of Lakeland, yet enjoying some excellent rural scenery, the area between Kendal and Windermere offers opportunities for pleasant walking where you may have things to yourself for long periods of time. If only the same could be said of the award-winning pubs. This circular walk offers flexibility since there are two half circuits of about the same length either side of Staveley with its frequent bus and rail services. Nowhere is it technically demanding and navigation is fairly straightforward.

Start the walk at Ings, a small hamlet on the A91 road halfway between Kendal and Windermere. Across the road from the well-known Watermill Inn and adjacent to the eastbound bus stop there is a lane running off to the north. Walk up this lane and in about 10 minutes you'll come across a bridleway leading off to the right. Navigation remains easy: ignore paths to right and left until you pass the buildings of Hugill Hall farm, and just after this, joining tarmac again, continue in more or less the same direction until you reach the heavily restored buildings of Heights Farm which look suspiciously like holiday lets in the making. A former resident

The Kentmere Valley near Staveley

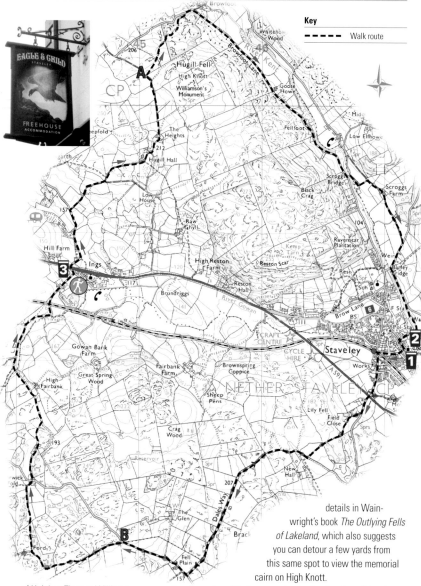

Key

- - - - - Walk route

of Heights, Thomas Williamson, apparently used to climb the nearby summit of High Knott daily before breakfast. His son had a monument erected in his honour in 1803.

Just after the bridleway bears left there's a step stile on your right (A, ⊕ 451002) which you take. A mile or so north west of here is the site of an early British settlement which antiquarians may wish to visit (⊕ 437009): there are more

details in Wainwright's book *The Outlying Fells of Lakeland*, which also suggests you can detour a few yards from this same spot to view the memorial cairn on High Knott.

Walk more or less in the direction of the signpost, staying quite close to the right-hand wall to find the next stile. Here some good views begin to open up over the upper reaches of the Kentmere Valley. You should be able to pick up a steadily improving track in the grass leading downhill through a gate, keeping the plantation on the far fellside straight ahead of you as you then join and follow the winding track down towards a quiet

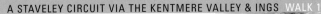

LEFT: **Scenery at Brackenthwaite** RIGHT: **A quiet corner in the Eagle & Child**

lane which you join via a gate. Simply continue downhill on this lane which turns sharply right near the valley foot (ignore the bridleway running off to the left) and follow the road for about a mile until you reach Scroggs Bridge. You're unlikely to meet traffic on this very quiet byway. Cross the bridge and bear immediately right on a footpath and then turn uphill by the cottages and join a wider bridleway where you turn right. Continue through the farmyard at Scroggs Farm on the bridleway and join another very quiet lane down towards the outskirts of Staveley by the river bridge. Don't cross the bridge but rather continue along on the road on the left bank of the river for about a quarter of a mile, then you'll see a signed footpath for Staveley on the riverside as the road veers away. There is evidence of former industry here at a weir, and in fact the industrial yards across the road contain the remains of the site of Staveley Mill, once an important wood-turning mill making bobbins. It was the owners of this mill who introduced a bill to Parliament to sanction the construction of the Kentmere reservoir, some miles up the valley, to ensure a reliable water supply to the mill. These days the mill yard is home to a small industrial and commercial estate which includes the new site of Hawkshead Brewery and its justifiably-popular Beer Hall, of which more in a moment!

Across the river on the obvious footbridge a short way downstream, follow the path towards the main road ahead; you'll be able to see the Eagle & Child pub over to your left, and the route as described here makes this our first port of call; if you want to visit the Hawkshead Beer Hall first either cut through the yard to the right of the path or turn right onto the main road and right again

close to the Spar grocery. The **Eagle & Child** 1 is a short walk down to the left, just across the river bridge. A winner of the coveted local CAMRA Pub of the Year award in 2007, it's easy to see why this large free house is a perennial favourite with discerning drinkers. The partially opened-out and atmospheric interior accommodates several distinct drinking areas, whilst all manner of ephemera line the walls and hang from the ceiling above the bar. Of more interest to us is the excellent range of well-kept beers with a strong local emphasis, dispensed from the five handpumps. Across the road (no longer a dangerous journey now the bypass has arrived) there's a lovely riverside beer garden. You'll get food here at luchtimes (until 2.30) and evenings.

Return along the village street, turn right by the Spar grocery, and into the industrial estate where the Hawkshead Brewery and **Beer Hall** 2 is right at the end, straight ahead of you. The showcase for the excellent brewery adjacent is an airy but pleasant space where you can sample a wide range of Hawkshead's brews. There are takeaway products, and even occasional beer festivals. The Beer Hall has an arrangement with the café next door so you can order your food there and have it brought to you. However, be aware of the evening closure (from 5pm) of the Beer Hall.

You can call it a day here if you wish by taking advantage of the buses and trains nearby, but to continue on the southern half of the route, return halfway back to the Eagle & Child, and take the footbridge over the stream and the road straight ahead which leads directly to Staveley railway station. Turn left here onto Crook Road, crossing the bypass, and look for a bridleway bearing off to the right shortly afterwards: it looks like slip road,

LEFT: **Bar at the Watermill, Ings** RIGHT: **The Beer Hall, Staveley**

and is tarred until you curve around the front of the higher houses when it becomes a grassy path winding up the knoll with fine views opening up behind you. The next section is very straightforward: simply follow this path until you turn sharp right at the Dales Way fingerpost just before a group of farm buildings, then follow this pleasant tarred but gated lane which you can expect to have to yourself. At the first junction turn right onto another quiet tarred road which climbs steeply, but with very good views opening up of the Pennines. Shortly after reaching the top of the brae look for a signed bridleway veering off to the left (B, ⊙ 448965) and take this. Gorse adds some attractive seasonal colour, and when you reach a couple of gates with a Dales Way sign pointing back the way you've come, go through the right-hand gate and continue in the same direction (keeping the wall on your left). A good track with fine views ahead reaches and curves around the plantation on your right and at the far end of the plantation (where the Dales Way continues directly ahead), take another bridleway right (signed to Borthwick Fold), which – with the trees behind a fence on your right – leads you down towards Borthwick Fold to emerge on the lane right by the farm. Turn right for few yards only and look for a footpath sign by the farm buildings across the road.

This path leads you along the edge of woodland, with fine views opening up towards Ambleside and Grasmere ahead, with the valley below. In about five minutes a step stile goes over the wall where it bends, taking you briefly into the plantation and out quickly via another step stile, and then downhill (with couple of guide posts to lead you) towards an unfenced tarred lane – award yourself an extra half pint if you emerge onto this by the wooden fingerpost! The Langdale Pikes and the Kentmere Fells further right are prominent in the view here and it's a pleasant spot to rest and drink in the view. Now it's simply a case of following this lane down and under the railway bridge: shortly afterwards it will conveniently deposit you right by the **Watermill Inn 3** at Ings, where we started. The Watermill is another pub of superlatives, winning the local CAMRA Pub of the Year gong in 2009 and awards from several other bodies. The heavily made-over interior retains some character: the flagged servery area is often crowded with punters eager to sample from the massive range (up to 16!) of real ales, many brewed on the premises, and very good too despite the rather silly names, mostly connected with the proprietors' pooch. Guests draw heavily on Cumbria's excellent portfolio of small brewers, and the pub serves food from an extensive menu all day until 9pm. The wall above the fireplace is adorned with so many CAMRA awards it's difficult to believe that anywhere else has any! Like the other pubs on this circuit, not to be missed.

Buses to Kendal and Windermere leave nearby on the main road.

PUB INFORMATION

1 Eagle & Child
Kendal Road, Staveley, LA8 9LP
01539 821320
www.eaglechildinn.co.uk
Opening Hours: 11-11; 12-10.30 Sun

2 Beer Hall
Hawkshead Brewery, Mill Yard, Staveley, LA8 9LR
01539 825260
www.hawksheadbrewery.co.uk
Opening Hours: 12-5 (6 Wed-Sun)

3 Watermill Inn
Ings, LA8 9PY
01539 821309
www.watermillinn.co.uk
Opening Hours: 12-11; 12-10.30 Sun

Grange to Cark via Hampsfell Hospice & Cartmel

WALK INFORMATION

Start: Grange-over-Sands railway station

Finish: Cark

Access: Rail to Grange (and route ends with access to Cark station). Bus X35 Kendal to Barrow stops by station. The useful 532 Grange Area Service serves Cark, Cartmel and Grange station

Distance: 5 miles (8km)

OS map: OS Explorer OL7

Key attractions: Hampsfell Limestone pavements; Hampsfell Hospice; Cartmel village and priory; Holker Hall

The pubs: King's Arms, Royal Oak, both Cartmel; Engine Inn, Cark. Try also: Pig & Whistle, Cartmel

An excellent linear walk with plenty of variety, making use of the good rail service along the south coast of Lakeland. A steady climb through pleasant woodland out of Grange leads to Hampsfell, an area of limestone pavement with its rare and distinctive habitat. The highest point of Hampsfell (also known as Hampsfield Fell) is 727 feet above sea-level; at the summit stands a curious hospice, located on an ancient pilgrimage route to the Cistercian monastery at Cartmel, with expansive views out across Morecambe Bay. Cartmel offers a variety of watering holes in an attractive village dominated by the 12th-century priory, before an easy walk across the racecourse leads into Cark where you can take refreshment in the Engine Inn before catching the train or bus back to Grange or points beyond.

Limestone pavement and windswept trees at the summit of Hampsfell

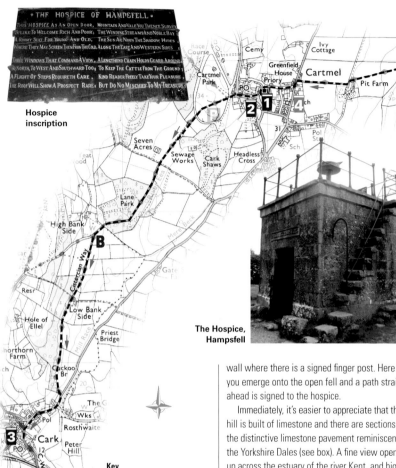

Hospice inscription

The Hospice, Hampsfell

Key

- - - - - Walk route

Coming out of the station pass the bus stand and walk up the road to the left. At the roundabout turn right into Windermere Road and head uphill past large houses on your left until you reach a footpath leading into the woods, signed 'Routen Well & Hampsfield'. This path takes you steadily uphill through the coppiced Eggerslack Woods. Cross a small lane following the footpath sign to Hampsfield fell. Further up you get to a complex junction with several paths meeting by an old retaining wall no doubt linked to the old limestone works which once dotted the fell; but simply continue ahead uphill and eventually the gradient eases and you reach a

wall where there is a signed finger post. Here you emerge onto the open fell and a path straight ahead is signed to the hospice.

Immediately, it's easier to appreciate that this hill is built of limestone and there are sections of the distinctive limestone pavement reminiscent of the Yorkshire Dales (see box). A fine view opens up across the estuary of the river Kent, and higher up you'll be able see the long railway causeway which crosses the estuary on its way to Arnside, as well as the famous (or infamous) sands of Morecambe Bay, especially if the tide is low. The path rises gently uphill and meets a straight wall. This is one of several walls dating back to the early nineteenth century, dividing the fell into a series of parcels of land or 'allotments' under an Act of Parliamentary Enclosure.

Cross over this by the stile and more or less follow the line of the wall, and in no time the curious hospice comes into view on the summit of Hampsfell (A, ⊙ 399794). The current building dates from 1846, erected by the Reverend T. Remington "for the use of visitors and others". Outside is an inscription in Greek which translates as 'rosy

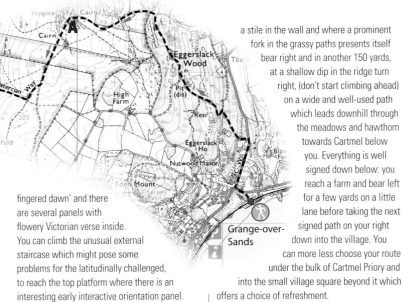

fingered dawn' and there are several panels with flowery Victorian verse inside. You can climb the unusual external staircase which might pose some problems for the latitudinally challenged, to reach the top platform where there is an interesting early interactive orientation panel.

Leave the hospice at more or less a 90 degree angle to your point of arrival, heading just west of south, aiming (in clear weather) for Humphrey Head, the peninsula jutting prominently out to sea (see walk 18). Cross the limestone pavement with its windblown and stunted trees, go through a stile in the wall and where a prominent fork in the grassy paths presents itself bear right and in another 150 yards, at a shallow dip in the ridge turn right, (don't start climbing ahead) on a wide and well-used path which leads downhill through the meadows and hawthorn towards Cartmel below you. Everything is well signed down below: you reach a farm and bear left for a few yards on a little lane before taking the next signed path on your right down into the village. You can more less choose your route under the bulk of Cartmel Priory and into the small village square beyond it which offers a choice of refreshment.

Enjoying an enviable position at the top of Cartmel's pretty village square (sadly choked by parked vehicles much of the time) lies the **King's Arms 1**. A fine building inside and out, it offers two comfortable rooms as well as a dining area to the rear overlooking the pretty little river Eea.

THE GRANGE LIMESTONE PAVEMENTS

Limestone has been quarried from the Grange-over-Sands district for centuries, and there are still the remains of the quarries and kilns across the hillside. However, the real geological jewels in the crown are the sections of limestone pavement.

There are only about ten square miles of limestone pavement in the United Kingdom, and very little in Lakeland, so it's a rare geological formation and habitat. Unfortunately the pavements here at Grange were very badly damaged throughout the 20th century by quarrying for clints (the blocks of limestone in between the weathered fissures, or grikes). The good news is that the Hampsfell pavements were the first in England to be designated with a Limestone Pavement protection order following new legislation in the 1981 Wildlife and Countryside Act.

Limestone pavements are a distinctive habitat: the deep grikes are home to ferns and other plants which thrive in a rocky but sheltered environment. Over 20 butterfly species, including the elusive High Brown Fritillary are recorded here. Pavements are renowned as being an excellent habitat for butterflies. A number of notable moth species have also been recorded, including the Speckled Yellow, Thyme Pug, Juniper Carpet and Mullein Wave. Badgers, stoats, weasels and brown hares live here and even a few red squirrels although these are now scarce. You can find out more about pavements at www.limestone-pavements.org.uk

LEFT: **The King's Arms, Cartmel**   RIGHT: **The Royal Oak, Cartmel**

Wooden beams abound. Appealing and often locally sourced food is available to accompany your ale, which comes from four handpumps. Expect a couple of Hawkshead beers and probably Tag Lag from Barngates. There's a pleasant seating area at the front of the pub for those sunny days…

Just a few yards away and also fronting the square, lies the **Royal Oak 2**. This place has lots of character, which has been carefully retained despite modernisation. Flagstones and old floorboards are complemented by plenty of low beams, and there's a lovely riverside garden at the back of the pub. Again there are four beers to choose from, Black Sheep Bitter, Marston's Pedigree, and two changing guests. Once again food is served lunchtimes and evenings.

It's possible that once installed in Cartmel you may find the prospect of another couple of miles walking less than alluring and decide to stay for another beer. The **Pig & Whistle 4** with its small snug bar is worth a visit in this case – it's away from the touristy centre towards the east end of the village and serves Robinson's beers.

For the hardy walkers, leave Cartmel at the opposite end of the square from the pubs, just to the left the of the prominent Cartmel sticky toffee pudding shop (!) This in turn leads you directly on to the racecourse which the Bridleway crosses, bearing gently left through a gate. The good bridleway leads through a pleasant wide valley and shortly into a woodland area; this in turn reaches a tarmac lane at a fork where we bear left (B, ⦿, 368779). For culture vultures, Holker Hall stately home and gardens is half a mile by the right fork.

Good views can be had back across to Hampsfell as this easy bridleway brings you out on to road at the outskirts of Cark. Turn right and walk into the village, taking care since there is no footway and there is an adverse blind bend – it may be sensible to cross the road. Cark is a small village and it would be completely impossible to miss the last pub of the route, the **Engine Inn 3** with its prominent white gable end. The pub was named after the steam engines which worked mills here in Cark. A recently refurbished free house offering two changing beers, you may be interested in the very decent Belgian beer menu here too, and it's worth knowing that the separate restaurant offers local produce like shellfish from Morecambe Bay. The Engine also does accommodation – ring ahead to check.

From the pub the bus stop is almost opposite, and the railway station is a very short walk further along road, but of course the advice is to check the times before settling down to your pint.

PUB INFORMATION

1 King's Arms
The Square, Cartmel,
LA11 6QB
015395 36220
Opening Hours: 11-11; 12-10.30

2 Royal Oak
The Square, Cartmel,
LA11 6QB
015395 36259
www.royaloakcartmel.co.uk
Opening Hours: 11.30-12.30

3 Engine Inn
Station Road, Cark in Cartmel,
LA11 7NZ
015395 58341
www.engineinn.co.uk
Opening Hours: 11.30 (12 Sun)-1.30am

TRY ALSO:

4 Pig & Whistle
Cartmel, LA11 6PL
015395 36482
Opening Hours: 5.30-11; 2-11 Fri; 12-11 Sat; 12-10.30 Sun

LINK Bus 532 or train to Kents Bank for walk 18, 2 miles. Train to Ulverston (walk 19), 8 miles. Bus X35 from Grange to Haverthwaite for walk 7 (8 miles).

Humphrey Head

Humphrey Head ends with a whimper rather than a bang...

Outside the national park and poking out into Morecambe Bay, the curious limestone headland of Humphrey Head sits at the extremity of one of the Furness peninsulas, and with the sand, mud and marshes of the bay on either side the walk is an airy one with excellent coastal views. Interest is added by virtue of the very different western and eastern sides of the promontory, the former exposed, high and open, the latter lower and thickly wooded. The last wolf in England was reputedly killed at Humphrey Head in the 15th century; the weather vane on Cartmel Priory close by depicts a wolf's head in recognition of this. Allithwaite, where the Pheasant Inn sits on a prominent site, is a quiet village with a bus service and conveniently close to the headland, making this an attractive half-day walk which can be combined with all or part of walk 17 if you want to extend the walking and drinking.

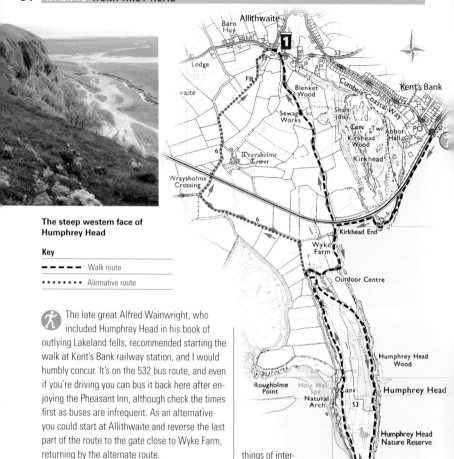

The steep western face of
Humphrey Head

Key

– – – – – Walk route

•••••••• Alernative route

The late great Alfred Wainwright, who
included Humphrey Head in his book of
outlying Lakeland fells, recommended starting the
walk at Kent's Bank railway station, and I would
humbly concur. It's on the 532 bus route, and even
if you're driving you can bus it back here after enjoying the Pheasant Inn, although check the times
first as buses are infrequent. As an alternative
you could start at Allithwaite and reverse the last
part of the route to the gate close to Wyke Farm,
returning by the alternate route.

In all but the highest tides and storms it's a
pleasant and easy walk along the side of the railway line from the station, keeping to the edge of
the marsh which here is firm and easy to traverse.
The wooded leeward side of the headland beckons
attractively in front of you. Birdwatchers may find

things of inter-
est here as the
marshes are wide
and extensive. As the
map shows, you leave
the railway briefly around a small promontory but
rejoin it before reaching the gate by Wyke Farm.

**Salt marsh and creeks from the summit ridge
of Humphrey Head**

The wooded eastern flank of Humphrey Head

Keep close to the stony foot of the railway embankment on this section to avoid any boggy areas and avoid the temptation to stray onto the marsh. At the point where a path joins from under the railway line, bear left, keeping on the seaward side of the farm on the clear path. The whaleback shape of Humphrey Head lies ahead of you as you pass a line of hawthorn trees between dry land on one side and the marsh stretching away on your left. Leave the marsh shortly, obeying the footpath

sign which takes you through a gate onto a pleasant little walled lane fringed with hawthorn, which brings you up to a road where you bear left and then left again almost immediately into the road to the study centre. Don't go through the gate into the centre grounds but instead spot the right of way sign on the telegraph pole which points you along the grassy slope to the right running up onto Humphrey Head past the buildings of the study centre. At the end of the study centre fence bear half left and look out in about 100 yards for a couple of wooden posts with white paint marks: these lead you down to a gate which runs into the woodland. The path through the woods is wide and clear, and the woodland floor is thickly carpeted with bluebells in spring.

Eventually leave the woodland by a rickety stile which opens out onto the grassy tip of the

WHAT TO SEE AT HUMPHREY HEAD NATURE RESERVE

Humphrey Head is a limestone promontory which is important both for its flora and fauna and for its geological exposures. The formal nature reserve of 23 hectares is a Site of Special Scientific Interest (SSSI) and covers the western cliffs and the open land, but not the woodland. The proximity to the sea and the limestone rock gives rise to an unusual combination of plants. The wind-bent trees are a feature – whitebeam and hawthorn being the dominant species. As regards plants, in spring look out for green-winged orchids and blue moorgrass. Look out in summer for spiked speedwell, limestone bedstraw, hoary and common rock rose,

and wild thyme. You may see peregrine falcons or ravens in summer, whilst in winter, coastal waders, shelducks, curlews, redshanks and snipe are common. Also at Humphrey Head is Holy Well spa, a natural spring accessible from the road below the cliffs. The aquifer is the source of the famous Holy Well of Cartmel Priory, renowned for its healing powers from the 1700s. The water is now bottled locally in Flookburgh as Willow Water, and is known to contain salicin – produced by rainwater washing through strata of white willow bark, built up over centuries. The company web site is gushing about the magical qualities of the water.

**Windblown hawthorn
trees on the exposed
ridge of Humphrey Head**

The Pheasant Inn, Allithwaite

headland, and it's then a simple walk down to the southernmost point which, rather unexpectedly, is not a sheer cliff but a gentle drop to sea level. It the tide is favourable it's quite safe to walk through the kissing gate and across the sand to the water's edge, and indeed it's possible at lower tides to return along the sandy shore underneath the cliffs and pick up a road back to the study centre. Either way this is a good spot to enjoy your flask and sandwiches if you have brought them. I would recommend as a better return route the airy walk which climbs up to the trig point at the summit of Humphrey Head, passing some severely mis-shapen trees – a testimony to the powerful winds which can sweep across this exposed headland. It's a surprisingly gentle ascent from the tip of the peninsula, and if you keep close to the fence on your left you'll get some fine views of the limestone cliffs on the seaward side of the head-land, and indeed of the wide sandy marshes and the mudflats which make this whole area such an interesting habitat. Returning via the summit ridge also offers fine views inland ahead of you with Hampsfield Fell (see walk 17) prominent.

Shortly the familiar study centre comes back into view and you can rejoin your out-ward route. At the point where you joined from Kent's Bank keep straight ahead on the path: it makes for the railway line which you cross under via an atmospheric little tunnel with barely enough headroom to walk through and the railway tracks just inches above your head – quite a noisy experience if a train is passing as you traverse! The right of way, part of the Cumbria Coastal Way, then heads more or less north inland through a series of gates and stiles (evidently not a very well walked section since the grass is quite long in places) before feeding into a farm lane and then in turn via a farmyard to bring you out right at the **Pheasant Inn 1**. If you started at Allithwaite and came out on this path and you cannot bear to tread the same way twice, you can follow the quiet lane from alongside the study centre (see alternate route on map) back into the village without encountering much traffic at all.

The Pheasant Inn sits prominently on a bend in the road: a former motel, the interior has been much modified, offering a choice of sitting areas and a lounge at the front with extensive views. On the bar Thwaites Original is joined by up to two changing guests. Call ahead for food finishing times but expect lunch and evening service.

PUB INFORMATION

1 Pheasant Inn
Allithwaite, CA13 9YE
017687 76234
www.the-pheasant.co.uk
Opening Hours: 11.30-2.30,
5.30-10.30 (11 Fri & Sat); 12-
2.30, 6-10.30 Sun

> **LINK** Cark and Cartmel (see walk 17) are both about two miles away and you may fancy extending your drinking by taking bus 532 to one or the other.

A Kendal town trail

WALK INFORMATION

Start/Finish: Kendal railway station (or bus station)

Access: Trains to Kendal from Windermere, Oxenholme and Lancaster. Bus 555 Lancaster to Keswick, X35 from Barrow and Furness, 567 from Kirkby Lonsdale; other local services

Distance: 2.5 miles (4km)

OS map: OS Explorer OL7

Key attractions: Kendal Castle; Quaker tapestry (in Meeting House); Abbot Hall Art Gallery and Museum of Lakeland Life; Museum of Natural History and Archaeology; Brewery Arts Centre; Serpentine Woods

The pubs: Castle Inn, Ring O' Bells, Rifleman's Arms, Miles Thompson, Burgundy's Wine Bar, Sanctuary Bar (Riverside Hotel), all Kendal

Lakeland's largest town is for many visitors simply a point of transit *en route* to places further into the national park. Indeed it's got very good transport links, although probably too many roads and vehicles, but the 'auld grey town' as it was known on account of the limestone buildings, is still very much worth a visit in its own right. It's been knocked around badly by the 'planners' over the years but they haven't been able to destroy all the history here – and there remain some fine buildings together with the views over the town from the two castle sites. The town's traditional trade was in wool, which gave the town its motto "*Pannus mihi panis*", or "wool is my bread". The variety of pubs on this interesting circuit vary from the staunchly traditional to the decidedly modern, with a plentiful range of ales to satisfy the choosiest visitor.

The walk starts at Kendal station, which may be the most logical point of arrival for eco-friendly pub goers. If you arrive at the bus station you can join the route by walking back down to the junction at Stramongate (see map). Head up Ann Street at the end of which the **Castle Inn 1** is just round to the right on Castle Street.

This traditional pub is a popular locals' haunt, away from both the commercial and tourist spots, and is well worth a visit. The carpeted interior

The Sanctuary Bar of the Riverside Hotel boasts a well-sited outdoor drinking terrace

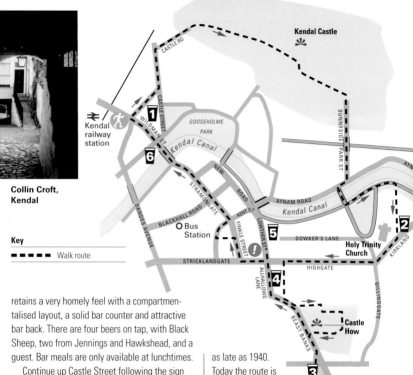

Collin Croft, Kendal

Key

■ ■ ■ ■ ■ Walk route

retains a very homely feel with a compartmentalised layout, a solid bar counter and attractive bar back. There are four beers on tap, with Black Sheep, two from Jennings and Hawkshead, and a guest. Bar meals are only available at lunchtimes.

Continue up Castle Street following the sign for the castle, and bear right into Castle Road. Just beyond the turn for Lower Castle Park there's an entrance into the castle grounds, and a path which ascends the hill towards the ruins which come into view ahead. Close to the northern entrance to the castle ruins there's an information plaque. Kendal Castle dates back to the time of the Norman barons; the earthwork on which the ruins now stand, surrounded by its deep ditch, was probably constructed in the late 12th century and may have had timber buildings and a small bailey to the north. The ruins consist of the remains of a curtain wall, three 13th-century towers and a 15th-century residential gatehouse.

At the far end of the ruins, follow the footpath directly down (towards the town) into Sunnyside. Walking down here you reach the bridge over the old Kendal Canal. Opened in 1819, the canal gave access to cheap coal from Lancashire opening the way to new steam-driven industrial developments. Although rendered largely obsolete by the coming of the railway soon afterwards, the canal stayed in use for delivering coal to Kendal gasworks until

as late as 1940. Today the route is used as a cycle track.

Beyond the bridge the road becomes Parr Street, named after Henry VIII's sixth and last wife who, according to legend, was born in Kendal Castle. Cross the busy one-way street and head over the river via the footbridge almost opposite. Turn left along the riverside here for a short distance, and just beyond the weir Church Walk runs off right to the imposing Holy Trinity parish church: the largest parish curch in Cumbria and only 3 feet narrower than York Minster! The church has five aisles and an 80-foot tower. In addition, culture vultures will be tempted to visit Abbot Hall with its gallery and museum on the right. Whatever your choice, refreshments are immediately to hand when you're done, for at the top of Church Walk by the road sits one of Kendal's venerable old inns, the **Ring O' Bells 2**.

An attractive building, it's likely that the inn was built around 1745. It had a famous sign dating back to 1814 representing the church tower below which bell ringers stood around a jug of ale. This original inn sign is now situated in the north aisle of the church, whilst a modern, rather glossy copy is mounted on the gable end of the inn itself. The pub has two bars, the smaller front bar patronised by the locals, with a larger lounge where the emphasis is upon food (except Thursday lunchtime). Between the two is a cosy snug bar served via a hatch with one long bench seat. Hawkshead Bitter and Thwaites Mild are joined in season by up to two changing guests.

Leaving the pub turn right and walk down Kendal's main street, the Highgate. Despite the traffic and the noise there's still much of architectural and historic interest on this fine road. Particularly noteworthy are the numerous small entries or yards which run off the streets on both sides. These were home to a variety of manufacturing industries, particularly on your right-hand side, down towards the river, where there were weaving shops and dyeing works. Many of the yards have nothing of interest remaining, but some are well worth a look.

Continue along the Highgate until just before the HSBC Bank, where we turn left into Collin Croft. This yard owes its development to a spring running down from the fell above. Taking advantage of the copious water supply at one time there was a currier (leather processor), a maltkiln and a brewery together in this yard, along with other workshops employing a range of craftsman. There was even an old beer house, the Malt Shovel. At the top end of the yard bearing round to the right there's a Civic Society plaque on wall just before you enter a covered passage which takes you up onto Beast Banks.

Turning left uphill past the Black Swan, a few yards further uphill will bring you to Garth Heads on your left: an ancient lane which once marked

Branthwaite Brow, Kendal

the line of a series of springs issuing from the limestone on the fellside above you. Taking this, climb the second flight of steps on the right, from which there's a good view across the valley with the parish church prominent and Kendal Castle. This grassy knoll you're on, now known as Castle Howe, is the site of the town's first Norman castle. Walk up and climb the steps to the obelisk built in 1788. You'll need to return down the knoll to continue on the path and exit further up Beast Banks.

Continue uphill passing first a green on the opposite side, then one ahead as the road splits. Here, on the right-hand side of the green, stands the next pub on our route, the **Rifleman's Arms** **3**. A handsome double-fronted building in a terrace, this friendly locals' pub which is a good supporter of local events, offers up to four mainly local ales in good condition. Note however that during the week the pub only opens at 6pm.

Leaving the pub simply retrace your steps down Beast Banks and continue downhill beyond the exit from Collin Croft. On the right-hand side just beyond the very distinctive old building with its chimney is the **Miles Thompson** **4**; yet another imaginative conversion by Wetherspoons. Opened in 1864, Shearman House as it was then called, was erected by local philanthropists as a public wash-house and baths, for the purpose of making wash-day more bearable for working people (mothers probably) living in Kendal's poorly ventilated cottages. Designed by local architect Miles Thompson, it included two pioneering

Bridge over the former Kendal Canal

LEFT: **The Castle Inn** RIGHT: **Impressive facade of the Miles Thompson**

spin-dryers. In addition there were eight large porcelain baths, the lowest charge for a warm bath being for two young women sharing: 3d (about 1p) each! The chimney is 70 feet (about 20 metres) high. Expect the usual JDW fare but with plenty of interesting beer choice.

Upon leaving the Miles Thompson walk down to the road junction. Directly ahead is the narrow one-way Lowther Street. Halfway down this road on the right (although it can also be accessed by turning right back onto Highgate and taking the first yard entry on the left) is **Burgundy's Wine Bar 5**. Despite the name this is much more a pub than a wine bar: an interesting listed building (recently extended at the rear) on split levels, it offers four real ales on draught, one of which is usually Yates' Fever Pitch. Expect them to be well-kept as Burgundy's is a *Good Beer*

Guide regular. In addition there's a decent range of continental beers, mainly in bottle. If you're in on Thursdays you'll catch some live music.

Return to Highgate and turn right, walking along as far as Finkel Street where you bear right again and look out for the narrow entry into New Shambles on the left, with its interesting shopfronts; then right into the market place and right down Branthwaite Brow, which is still an attractive street with several fine buildings. Turn left at the bottom, and now simply head straight down Stramongate to the river, crossing busy Blackhall Road by the lights. Our last port of call is immediately across the bridge – and if it's a fine day you'll be able to see if there are any seats left on the small but perfectly placed riverside terrace at the **Sanctuary Bar 6** in the Riverside Hotel. The hotel is a modern conversion of an old mill – it's been done well but inside the bar area is almost too posh with decadent sofas and easy chairs abounding. As you'd expect you can get a meal here, but the real draw for us is the well-kept brace of beers from the excellent Hawkshead Brewery.

The station is just ahead, the bus station back down Stramongate and right into Blackhall Road.

LINK Walk 15 (Scout Crag & Sizergh) also starts from Kendal. Walk 16, via bus 555 (approx hourly) to Ings (5 miles). Walk 13 via bus 567 to Kirkby Lonsdale (13 miles).

PUB INFORMATION

1 Castle Inn
Castle Street, Kendal, LA9 7AA
01539 729983
Opening Hours: 11.30-midnight (1am Sat)

2 Ring O' Bells
39 Kirkland, Kendal, LA9 5AF
01539 720326
Opening Hours: 12-11 (10.30 Sun)

3 Rifleman's Arms
4 Greenside, Kendal, LA9 4LD
01539 723224
Opening Hours: 6 (12 Sat & Sun)-midnight

4 Miles Thompson
Allhallows Lane, Kendal, LA9 4JH
01539 815710
Opening Hours: 9-11 (midnight Fri & Sat)

5 Burgundy's Wine Bar
19 Lowther Street, Kendal, LA9 4DH
01539 733803
www.burgundyswinebar.co.uk
Opening Hours: 11.30-3.30 (not Tue & Wed), 6.30-midnight; 11-midnight Sat; closed Mon

6 Sanctuary Bar
(Riverside Hotel)
Stramongate Bridge, Kendal, LA9 6EL
01539 734861
www.riversidekendal.co.uk
Opening Hours: 11-11

Derwent & Buttermere Group – the North West

View over Borrowdale to Derwent Water and Skiddaw from Castle Crag

Buttermere round

WALK INFORMATION

Start/Finish: Buttermere village, by the Bride Hotel

Access: Summer bus 77A from Keswick

Distance: 3.4 miles (5.4km)

OS map: OS Explorer OL4

Key attractions: Honister *Via Ferrata* (1.5 miles); Buttermere Lake; Crummock Water; hill walking

The pubs: Fish Inn, Bridge Hotel, both Buttermere

Buttermere village

Buttermere is one of the more secluded parts of Lakeland lying between two of the quieter larger lakes, Buttermere itself and Crummock Water. Despite being fairly accessible from Keswick it retains its rural atmosphere mainly because there's actually very little here apart from a couple of hotels both of which, happily, offer a range of real ales. There are no shops and, apart from the fine scenery in all directions, not much in the way of tourist 'honeypots' although the new Honister development with its *Via Ferrata* climbing route is an interesting if rather pricey recent attraction. The walk here offers a valley climb and an easy saunter along a grassy ridge with excellent views before descending to the lake shore and following the Mill Beck back into the village. Take care descending from the summit of the ridge down to Crummock Water – the path, although well defined, is steep and you may need your hands. There is an alternative valley descent.

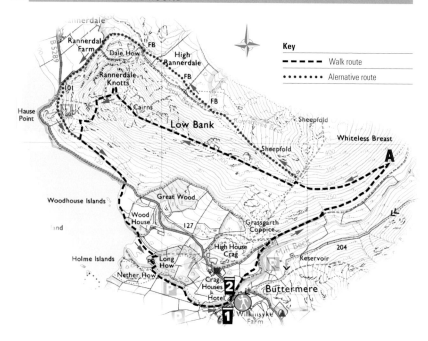

Key

━ ━ ━ ━ Walk route

• • • • • • • Alernative route

From the Bridge Hotel at the centre the village, take the signed footpath right across the street which immediately takes you onto a delightful wooded path climbing steadily but very pleasantly through the trees alongside the rushing water of Mill Beck. It's the sort of start to a walk that immediately puts you in a good mood.

On the fells above Buttermere village

The path climbs up to bring you in about a quarter of a mile to a wooden gate accessed by some steps on your left. This joins another path which we follow upstream. Across the valley the small lane which runs over the pass into Newlands and thence on to Portinscale and Keswick can be seen snaking up the hill. Fork left onto the higher of the two paths in a few minutes where the fence gives away to a wall. It feels very much as if you're walking into the wilderness here with fells all around. At the point where a small beck below you runs down the fellside opposite and joins the main stream on your right with a ruined sheepfold at the confluence, look for a path doubling back up the hill at a very oblique angle (A, ⊕ 186178). You're now looking at the high ridge walling the southwestern side of

Buttermere Lake: Red Pike, High Crag and High Stile. A little further on, views open up over Buttermere village below.

Shortly you'll arrive at a junction of paths: the one crossing ours at right angles drops steadily back down to the village on your left or steeply uphill towards Whiteless Pike on your right. Ahead of you, our route climbs gently onto the distinct ridge of Low Bank running towards the crags of Rannerdale Knotts. If the weather has closed in a little and/or you don't fancy the fairly steep descent from the end of the ridge ahead, a good lower level alternative is the well trodden and easy-to-follow track a few yards to the right, which runs down into the valley with views beyond of Crummock Water and Loweswater. (If you select this alternative, bear left at the low ground near the lake, ensuring you keep to the left of the stream as you approach the lowland. This enables you to rejoin the main route via the B5289 road along the lake shore).

If the weather is good there is no other reason to forgo the pleasant ridge ahead of you: easy walking rising slowly with fine views all around particularly over the lakes, until at the summit at

The final part of the route follows the beck back into Buttermere village

the further end there is a steep descent which winds down to the left, where care is needed. This will bring you via some stepped sections where conservation workers have made things

Looking across the head of Crummock Water from the fells above Buttermere

LEFT: **The Fish at Buttermere** RIGHT: **Early morning sunshine lights up the Bridge Hotel**

rather easier, down towards a wide grassy bridleway. Bear left onto this and allow it to lead you gently down to the road towards a stand of pine trees, by the lakeshore almost opposite a gated footpath.

Take this path down to the shore of Crummock Water, and follow this lakeside path around the wooded headland. Once around here and through a gate in the bay, strike away from the shore on a grassy path close to the fence, across the meadow. This leads via another gate onto a path skirting a second wooded outcrop. Turn right along this path and in 200 yards or so, after joining a stream on the right, cross this on the footbridge and continue in the same direction along the stream, now on your left (signed 'Footpath to Buttermere Village and Scale Bridge'). This excellent finale to the route returns you to the village very quickly, and passing the idyllic-looking camp site on your left you arrive at the **Fish Inn** [1].

Also known as the Fish Hotel, alterations over the years have resulted in the loss of some of its 'pubby' atmosphere. Nonetheless, the carpeted bar has an enviable view out over the fells; and the best news of all is the excellent range of cask ales: three from Jennings including the popular Sneck Lifter, complemented by three rotating guest beers with local Cumbrian brewers like Keswick and Hesket Newmarket prominent. As with the Bridge Hotel up the road the Fish offers a wide menu at lunchtimes and evenings. Mary Robinson (1778–1837), the 'Maid of Buttermere' who is buried in Caldbeck churchyard (see walk 27) was the daughter of the landlord of the Fish Inn. She was the subject of Melvyn Bragg's novel of that name.

It's a short step up the road to the **Bridge Hotel** [2]: you'll probably have recognised by now the old mill building where you started, annexed as part of the hotel, which was first licensed as a coaching inn as long ago as 1735. Although opened out, the walkers' bar retains a pub atmosphere with a dining room adjacent. Once more you can expect a good range of beers with Theakston Old Peculier and Black Sheep alongside the house beer Buttermere Bitter, brewed by Hawkshead, whose Lakeland Gold completes the menu.

PUB INFORMATION

[1] **Fish Inn**
Buttermere, CA13 9XA
017687 70253
www.fishhotel.com
Opening Hours: 10.30-3, 6-11; 11-11 Sat & Sun; closed Jan

[2] **Bridge Hotel**
Buttermere, CA13 9UZ
017687 70252
www.bridge-hotel.com
Opening Hours: 10.30-11 (10.30 Sun)

> **LINK** Walk 25 via summer bus 77A to stop at Beck House (4 miles). Walk 22 via summer bus 77 to Seatoller (5 miles).

Around Catbells & Newlands to Braithwaite

WALK INFORMATION

Start/Finish: Portinscale, at road junction by tea rooms

Access: Bus 77A/86 or walk from Keswick to Portinscale (¾ mile)

Distance: 6.9 miles (11km)

OS map: OS Explorer OL4

Key attractions: Fawe Park and Lingholme; Catbells; Keswick attractions (¾ mile)

The pubs: Coledale Inn, Middle Ruddings Country Inn, both Braithwaite. Try also: Derwent Lodge, Portinscale

The wooded western shore of Derwentwater is the start of this varied walk which then diverts inland (with an option to climb the popular lakeside fell of Catbells) into the rural valley of Newlands. The route then skirts the lower slopes of Barrow Fell into Braithwaite, a fell-edge village now bypassed by the main road. Aim for an early start if you're intending to take in the ascent of Catbells *en route*, since the walk is on the long side even without this extra detour. The route can be shortened to about 5 miles by catching the bus from Braithwaite back to Portinscale or Keswick. Be warned that the 2009 floods destroyed both the footbridge and road bridge over the Newlands and Coledale Becks respectively, close to Braithwaite, but work is well in hand to repair these and all should be back to normal by the time you come to walk – if not there will be a warning in the village and you will need to go by the lane instead (see alternative route on map).

View across the rooftops of Braithwaite towards Skiddaw

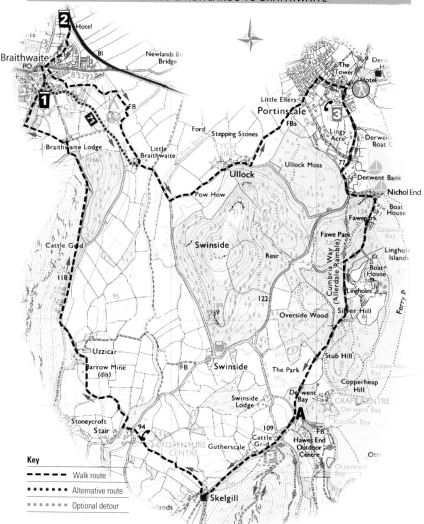

Key

‒ ‒ ‒ ‒ Walk route

• • • • • • Alternative route

• • • • • • Optional detour

Start in Portinscale – in summer, Honister Rambler bus 77A runs from Keswick and will drop you at Nichol End, just south of the village (see map) – otherwise, walk there from the village centre along the lane. Just at the point where the lane bears right, the footpath bears left through the trees to the boatyard on the lake shore. Don't confuse it with the footpath climbing southwards into the trees a further 40 yards on.

The waterside café, 'Downstairs @ Nichol End' is tucked into the bay here and feels like a long way from the bustle of Keswick High Street. The first mile of the walk continues through the mixed woodland with occasional lake views past the big houses at Fawe Park and Lingholm where Beatrix Potter holidayed and which provided the setting for some of her tales. Cross a clearing and a smaller woodland area and you emerge on the private road to the Hawes End Outdoor Centre (A, 248214). The path continues straight across and climbs up to join the motor road from Portinscale to Grange at the northern nose of Catbells in another 200 yards.

The road divides, the through road heading left on the lake side of the fell, while our route takes the no-through road to the right towards Skelgill.

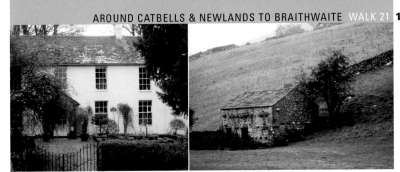

LEFT: **Skelgill farm** RIGHT: **A Lakeland field barn**

There's a well-trodden path between the two, heading directly up Catbells – and no wonder, since this well-loved hill offers delightful views across the lake and Newlands Valley to the fells beyond, out of all proportion to its height. It was one of Wainwright's favourites, even if he sometimes got exasperated by the sheer numbers of trippers on its ridge. The ridge path is straightforward to follow, but take a guidebook and/or map and allow at least an hour to climb to the top and return to the same point to continue the walk.

Back on the main route, follow the narrow road marked Skelgill until the tarmac runs out at Skelgill Farm – an attractive building in a charming secluded spot at the foot of the open fell above. Go through the gate and follow the tarred road round to the right, downhill, to emerge in less than half a mile at the tiny hamlet of Stair. Here go straight ahead, passing the Newlands Adventure Centre, a former mill, and across the bridge, where immediately on the right is a signed path to Uzzicar farm. The path is well marked but look for the waymarks which lead up to the farm, in a great rural location.

Catbells in silhouette across Derwentwater

Walk up the farm road to the unfenced lane above, under the slopes of Barrow Fell. Turn right and walk along the lane for a couple of hundred yards before forking off to the left on a very clear bridleway which climbs the hill obliquely to the upper boundary of the plantation ahead. There are good views across the vale to the wooded slopes of Swinside and the first part of the walk across to your right. In a few minutes you'll arrive at Braithwaite Lodge. Look for the footpath at 90-degrees left here, rather than the bridleway straight ahead. Crossing two fields you then drop down into a narrow wooded ravine and across the tiny Barrow Gill on a footbridge. At the road by the pink house above, simply turn right and walk down 250 yards to the **Coledale Inn** 1 sited on a bluff overlooking the loose-knit village of Braithwaite.

This historic inn, once a pencil factory, has been extended and modernised but still has some character, notably in the oak bar counter. A long-standing outlet for the straw-coloured Yates Bitter, the guest beers are frequently from the nearby Keswick brewery. There's a separate room where the emphasis is on food. In good weather

LEFT: **Coledale Inn, Braithwaite** RIGHT: **Middle Ruddings Country Inn, Braithwaite**

the beer garden offers fine views, with the bulk of Skiddaw filling the eastern sky.

A small footpath immediately below the pub leads down to the village shop and left across the stream to the Royal Oak, which is the other village pub (Jennings beers). But the other featured stop here is ¼ mile further on: turn right by the Royal Oak then fork left to take the road leading to the A66 Workington road (not right past the pub car park down to A66 in the Keswick direction). Where you meet the dual carriageway, the **Middle Ruddings Country Inn** sits on the left above the road. This is a comfortable small hotel with an open fire in the main bar and good views from the windows across to Skiddaw. The draw here is however not the interior but the well-kept range of changing guest beers, with up to three to choose from. Expect the beers to be locally sourced. There's a pleasant terraced garden outside with the one downside that you're uncomfortably close to the busy and noisy A66 road.

There are buses back to Keswick from Braithwaite if you want to call it a day here: the X5 is the most frequent. Continuing, retrace your steps to the Royal Oak with good views of the fells ahead. Cut through the alley immediately left of the pub to emerge on another lane with a footpath more or less directly across. This is where any warning on the footbridge ahead (see introduction) should be posted. Assume no news is good news! If you do need to detour, turn

right beyond the footpath and then left at the lane leading over the stream, following this to Little Braithwaite (see map).

Our path follows a raised bank along the stream side as it skirts the camp site, crossing the small beck on a footbridge (we hope!) and emerging on the lane at Little Braithwaite farm, where the lane from Braithwaite re-joins our route. Follow the lane across the river on a new bridge built to replace one swept away in the 2009 floods, and turn left on the even quieter lane to Ullock in 200 yards further. Views are good throughout.

At the far end of the hamlet of Ullock a footpath drops down left and leads through the fields and low-lying farmland before climbing up onto the rocky knoll on which Portinscale is built. The right of way leads past the rambling suburban houses and reaches a lane. Turn right, and this brings you back to the road T-junction in Portinscale by the tea rooms. On the right, beyond the tea rooms, the **Derwent Lodge** , which you passed at the start, is the best bet if you want another beer: three real ales, two from Jennings. Otherwise/afterwards take the no-through road past the Derwentwater Hotel to the suspension bridge at the end of the village street. The footpath back onto Keswick (¾ mile) is signed shortly beyond leading across the meadow to the right.

LINK From Keswick to Seatoller for walk 22 via Route 78 Borrowdale bus (7 miles).

PUB INFORMATION

1 Coledale Inn
Braithwaite, CA12 5TN
017687 78272
www.coledale-inn.co.uk
Opening Hours: 11-11; 12-11 Sun

2 Middle Ruddings Country Inn
Braithwaite, CA12 5RY
017687 78436
www.middle-ruddings.co.uk
Opening Hours: 12-1

TRY ALSO:

3 Derwent Lodge
Portinscale, CA12 5RF
017687 73145
www.derwentlodgehotel.co.uk
Opening Hours: 11-midnight (11 Sun)

Upper Borrowdale & Castle Crag, via Seatoller & Rosthwaite

WALK INFORMATION

Start/Finish: Seatoller

Access: Bus 77A/78 from Keswick

Distance: 4.75 miles (7.5km)

OS map: OS Explorer OL4

Key attractions: The Bowder Stone; *Via Ferrata* at Honister Pass

The pubs: Riverside Bar (Scafell Hotel), Rosthwaite; Honister Yew Tree, Honister Pass

A short circular walk in arguably Lakeland's most beautiful (certainly one of the most heavily wooded) valleys, with the strongly recommended option to climb one of Lakeland's easiest fells: Castle Crag. The natural environment abounds in glacial features straight from the pages of your old geography textbook – and in Rosthwaite the effortlessly handsome stone cottages positively nestle amid truly stunning scenery, attractive at any time of year. The route starts by climbing quite steeply onto a terrace above the valley floor before the climb to Castle Crag, which although not even 1,000 feet still requires some care and respect on the steep final section across old quarry waste. (Those who don't fancy the climb can omit this part and spend more time in the pub!) Then you descend to the village – returning along the riverside via the small hamlet of Longthwaite. Paths are generally in very good condition but, as usual, care is required and some sections may be wet.

Derwentwater in the early morning

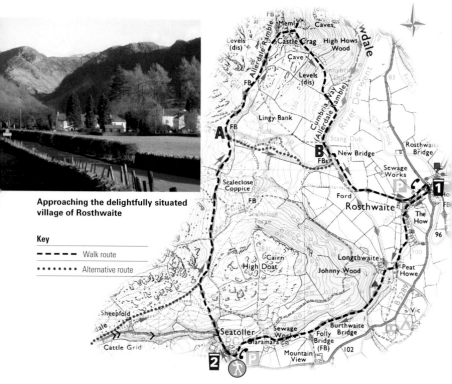

Approaching the delightfully situated village of Rosthwaite

Key

— — — — Walk route

• • • • • • • Alternative route

If you're starting in Keswick, the obvious access point (unless you're already in Borrowdale), pick up the useful Borrowdale bus 77, which runs frequently throughout the day, and take it right down to the terminus at Seatoller, admiring the wonderful scenery on the way. In summer, a new service, the 77A, continues over the pass to Buttermere. Another option is to take this bus and alight half a mile beyond Seatoller, by the bridleway just beyond the cattle grid (see map), which cuts out the initial steep climb.

Seatoller itself is a charming hamlet of old farmers' and miners' cottages at the foot of the steep pass up to Honister and over to Buttermere. If you have a fondness for the Lakeland vernacular architecture and are visiting Seatoller for the first time you'll find it hard to leave.

We start by getting one of the two climbs out of the way straightaway. Walk up through the hamlet, and as the road steepens and at the point where it turns sharply left, go through the gate ahead and take the path which strikes straight up the fellside for a short distance before joining the wide Allerdale Ramble path which we join by turning right. If the terrain looks confusing simply continue uphill until you join a wide and well-worn track with steeper, craggier ground above. The path keeps to the 250m contour northwards through a pass before a fine view soon opens up to the right, and ahead towards the wooded hill of Castle Crag and the 'Jaws of Borrowdale' which no less than the late great Alfred Wainwright called the loveliest square mile in Lakeland. I wouldn't argue with that.

As you scan right, Rosthwaite is visible in the valley below: but on reaching Tongue Gill where the path from the village crosses ours, pause awhile (A, ⊙ 245153). Looking up, you can pick out the spoil heaps which make the remains of Rigghead slate quarry. For us it's decision time: if it's raining or the mist is down, you may have an excuse not to press on to Castle Crag — otherwise, unless you haven't the stamina, I would enthusiastically recommend you continue over the bridge on the path to the Crag. The path down to Rosthwaite – like all tracks hereabouts a delightful one – follows the gill down to the River Derwent to rejoin the main route (see point B on map).

Continuing on to Castle Crag, if it feels as if you're walking on a road (such is the quality of the path here) well, you are, or were, for this route originated to link the Rigghead quarries with the village of Grange, two miles north. But enjoy it while you can for soon, at a point just before the track crosses a small stream, a stile in the wall (right) marks the point where we leave to complete the final ascent to the summit of Castle Crag. It's a pretty straightforward route – through a couple of walls by stiles, and the final section (take care) through the remains of an old quarry with some slightly exposed steps before the final top is reached. The views are

Castle Crag in winter

excellent, especially north over Derwentwater to Skiddaw. Just below you, a plaque set into a large boulder celebrates the life of John Hamer, killed in the First World War, and ten other men of Borrowdale. John's father, Sir William Hamer, gave the Crag to the National Trust in 1920.

If (and it's a big if) the weather is fine you will be sorry to leave this top, but by now the pub will be open, and this is a pub walk. There is only one safe way off: the way you arrived, until the

GLACIATION IN BORROWDALE

Castle Crag is a good spot from which to observe the impact of the rivers of ice which shaped the landscape around you. To the south, the high mountains of Scafell and Great Gable mark the central dome of the Cumbrian mountains from which the glaciers radiated out, eroding and widening the old river valleys as they went. When the ice melted, lakes filled all the deep hollows – Derwentwater is one of those that has survived, and it's thought that the flat area around Rosthwaite was once a temporary lake. Streams like Tongue Gill, which tumble steeply down to the now-lower valley floors are the hanging valleys from your

school geography lessons. In a way though it's the smaller features that grab the interest. South of Rosthwaite, seen best on the path running south west from the village towards Longthwaite, are some fine roches moutonees, with their characteristic scratches where the ice rode over them; and a series of ridges across the valley floor marking the debris (or moraine) at the snout of the glacier as it retreated. The 'Jaws of Borrowdale' where you're standing was a particularly tough area of volcanic rock which resisted the ice before it continued north and gouged out the softer rocks underneath the modern Derwentwater.

Rosthwaite from the slopes of Castle Crag

LEFT: **Borrowdale in winter** RIGHT: **Inside the Riverside Bar**

Rosthwaite path branches off clearly left over another stile after a few minutes, after the zig-zag
through the old spoil heap. The path leads fairly
steeply downhill, with delightful views ahead to
Rosthwaite and the confluence of the two valleys
beyond it. You eventually join the short cut (B,
252151), where you cross the Derwent at
New Bridge. Then it's a few gentle minutes into
the village, passing the Flock-Inn tea shop in a
recently converted barn before reaching the main
road by the shop.

Before 1750, horse-drawn sledges provided
the only transport to Rosthwaite and it was not
until the 1840s that a road was constructed. That
road bypasses the old village street which you
ought to detour down and see, if you like Lakeland
cottages – here they are absurdly picturesque,
although the window police need to visit one or
two. The rest of you will head straight for the
pub (turn right at the main road). It's actually the
Riverside Bar to the rear of the Scafell
Hotel. This was, when the author first used it, a
very basic no-frills room with a
veranda where you could drink
above the roaring river under
a plastic roof, but it's been
updated. Nonetheless it still
provides a welcome to all who
come off the hill, and there
is still a real fire in winter. I
hope they remember that this
is a mountain area still, where
muddy boots and dripping
jackets should not be out of
place. No more 'improvements'
please!

The beer range is far better now than it was,
with several handpumps dispensing a changing
range of guest ales in addition to Black Sheep
and Theakston's bitters and Old Peculier. Expect
something from the nearby Keswick brewery, and
perhaps from Copper Dragon, the Skipton brewery.
The food is decent and still reasonably priced.

You can call it a day here and, if you need
to, return to Keswick by bus or cab, to return to
Seatoller, take the little lane right opposite the
hotel entrance, past some pretty cottages, and
just after it bears left in about 200 yards look for
a footpath sign off to the right (Longthwaite).
This in turn leads you left through a wall and
the path then crosses several fields to emerge
at Longthwaite, another hamlet by the river
Derwent. You join a small lane and, turning
right onto it, cross the river on a picturesque
bridge. The path then bears left to follow the
river in front of the youth hostel, and then into
an attractive wooded stretch never far from the
water. Ignore the path off left to the river at Folly
Bridge, and it's less than half
a mile to Seatoller. Here, the
picturesque **Honister Yew
Tree** in the village offers
a welcome end-point. This bar
was originally two cottages,
built in 1628. It's primarily an
eatery and café, but it nonetheless sells Jennings beers too
so it's an ideal and atmospheric
place to end up whilst waiting
for your bus to Keswick. Worth
checking opening times before
setting out though.

PUB INFORMATION

1 Riverside Bar
(Scafell Hotel)
Rosthwaite, Borrowdale Valley,
CA12 5XB
017687 77208
www.scafell.co.uk
Opening Hours: 11-11; 12-
10.30 Sun

2 Honister Yew Tree
Honister Pass, Borrowdale,
Keswick, CA12 5XN
017687 77634
Opening Hours: 10-5 winter;
11-11 summer; closed Mon

Bassenthwaite village & lake

Start/Finish: Bassenthwaite village

Access: Bus X4 Keswick-Workington stops at the Castle Inn on the A591. Caldbeck Rambler bus 73/73A, Saturdays and daily during school summer holidays

Distance: 6.4 miles (10.4km)

OS map: OS Explorer OL5

Key attractions: Mirehouse; St Bega's church

The pubs: Sun Inn, Bassenthwaite

The shore path at Bassenthwaite

Bassenthwaite is one of the larger lakes but is less well known than many. The western shore is now occupied by the busy A66, but conversely the eastern side of the lake is peaceful and attractive. One of the highlights of this walk is the shore path, where you can look out for the elusive Eachy, a submarine monster which a scientific expedition in 1961 failed to find. The steeply rising lower fells around the village make once again for a route of contrasts and there are fine views to be had, particularly on the first part of walk. There are some stretches of road walking but these follow narrow lanes which even in the tourist season carry very light traffic. One word of warning: after heavy rain some sections of the lakeside path are liable to be flooded, although not usually more than a couple of inches, and these can be by-passed. Suitable footwear is essential, for even in drier periods you're likely to encounter marshy areas.

Sun Inn sign at Bassenthwaite

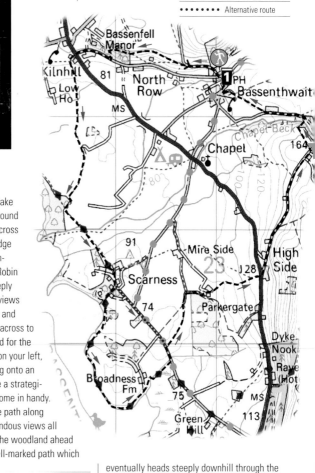

From the Sun Inn, take the lane running around the rear of the pub and across the small beck by the bridge – turning left and then immediately right (signed 'Robin Hood'), and climbing steeply up the hill, with the fine views back towards Ullock Pike and Skiddaw behind you and across to the lake: an ample reward for the toil. Taking the footpath on your left, close to the top, emerging onto an airy grassy terrace where a strategically placed seat might come in handy. Contour along the terrace path along the top fence with tremendous views all the way, until you enter the woodland ahead via a gate. Follow the well-marked path which

Lowland plain adjacent to the lake and close to Bassenthwaite village

eventually heads steeply downhill through the trees and joins the quiet lane at the bottom. Turn right and walk along to join the main A591 road in a few hundred yards. Just along the road to the right is the *Castle Inn* where the Keswick bus stops; it's possible to call in here for a coffee and a bite to eat, or even a glass of ale in the Lakers bar where Hesket Newmarket beers are the most likely to be on.

Back where you met the A591, pick up the footpath almost opposite the lane end, by Kilnhill Barn, and cross the road carefully. Through the gate into the camping ground, over the stile, and the right of way leads across a wide flat

Bassenthwaite village

landscape of meadows towards a white cottage on a knoll over a mile away in the distance. The Skiddaw massif and the closer Ullock Pike dominate the skyline. At a second metal gate, where the footpath sign points right, follow the edge of the fence right down, ignoring another stile, to cross a second stile in the far corner of the field. Follow the waymarks across some marshy ground to another gate, and continue on the faint path through the marsh in broadly the same direction towards the trees. White posts guide you, and once across the marsh the path

follows a well-trodden route along a stream before crossing it in about 100 yards. Obey the next footpath sign pointing towards the farm buildings in the trees, spotting the exit about 50 yards to the left of the house. Thereafter the path through the wooded grounds of Scarness is well signed. When you get to the entrance of the Bassenthwaite Lake Lodges, a signed path takes you sharply right to follow the lane along the side of the lodge wall right down to the lake shore at Scarness Bay.

For the next mile or so you'll have the lake as your very close companion (maybe too close if it's been raining heavily in the recent past) as you work your way around the headland of Broadness and into Bowness Bay. There are boardwalks and stepping stones in the most vulnerable places, but in extremis you may have to retrace your steps and follow the little lane instead (see map). It's a pity about the drone of traffic on the A66 on the opposite shore of the

Looking west to Grisedale Pike and the Grasmoor Fells

Sun Inn, Bassenthwaite

lake, but aside from this the location is very agreeable. The right of way then strikes inland (but look out for the signed path to right of the driveway, and don't end up at Broadness Farm) across a marshy wetland to join a narrow lane (A, 298225). Hopefully the flood damage at this point will have been repaired by the time you walk the route. Turn left and look out for the footpath to the right in about 150 yards through a couple of fields, keeping the woodland on your right to join a track in the far corner of the second field. Follow this good track round to the right and then look out for the footpath bearing off to the left by the buildings at Moorside. At this point you leave behind the flat lakeside lowlands and start climbing steadily up the hill towards the group of buildings ahead of you on the main road.

Several stiles later when you arrive there cross carefully, take the quiet lane opposite (signed 'Orthwaite') and follow this for about three-quarters of a mile (ignoring the first footpath sign to the left). Just after the brow of the hill and opposite a bridleway on the right, the footpath leaves the lane at 90-degrees left, and heads downhill towards a wooded river valley. It's easy to miss the path which heads off to the right as you reach the trees but once you've found it you are led unmistakably steeply downhill on a good track to cross the pleasant beck at the bottom and then to join another narrow lane shortly beyond. Follow this lane to the left past Burthwaite and look out for a footpath shortly beyond, which climbs steeply for about 50 yards to a stile beyond and then bears left. Follow the field boundary through into the next field by which time the village of Bassenthwaite is upon you. You will emerge by a small green: from here double back to your right along the lane and you'll soon arrive back at the **Sun Inn** 🔢. It's a well-sited Jennings housewith a sun-trap garden facing Ullock Pike and the lower slopes of Skiddaw. The opened-out interior is comfortable, and there's a separate, smaller games room. Expect up to four beers from the Jennings/Marston's list. The food is well regarded and includes locally-sourced ingredients.

For bus users the quickest way back to the Castle Inn and the X4 service is across the bridge again, and left along the quiet lane. If you don't fancy the return bus journey quite yet, the pub also offers food and four-star accommodation.

PUB INFORMATION

🔢 **Sun Inn**
Bassenthwaite, CA12 4QP
017687 76439
Opening Hours: 12 (4.30 Mon)-
11 (11.30 Fri & Sat)

A Cockermouth town trail

WALK INFORMATION

Start/Finish: Castlegate

Access: Buses X4 and X5 from Penrith and Keswick; other slower buses

Distance: 1 mile (1.5km); with detour 2 miles (3km)

OS map: OS Explorer OL4

Key attractions: Jennings Brewery; Wordsworth House; Kirkgate buildings; Cocker riverside path; Lakeland Sheep and Wool Centre

The pubs: Bush Hotel, Swan Inn, Bitter End, 1761, Castle Bar, all Cockermouth. Try also: Tithe Barn, Cockermouth

In my opinion Cockermouth is one of the finest of the Cumbrian towns: far less touristy than Keswick, more colourful than Kendal, and more attractive than Ambleside. It has a good number of solid and handsome buildings, many modest in stature but creating an agreeable ensemble; culture vultures will enjoy the Wordsworth connections; and importantly it's a good drinking destination with several fine pubs offering a wide and increasing range of beers. The welcome re-opening of Jennings brewery in early 2010 after the floods (see below) is a vote of confidence in the future of brewing here from owners Marston's, and there's no better place to drink the beers. And to name but one other highlight, in the Bitter End the town has a vibrant ex-brewpub with a good range of locally-brewed ales on offer.

Cockermouth took a huge hit in the 2009 floods and at the time of writing the town is still recovering. The Main Street in particular was devastated, and that goes for the pubs too in this low-lying part of the town. Happily some of the best pubs in town lie well above the flood plain and escaped the worst. That said, by the time you visit things should be more or less back to normal, and I'd recommend giving some of the other Main Street pubs a try in addition to those on this circuit.

Cockermouth Main Street

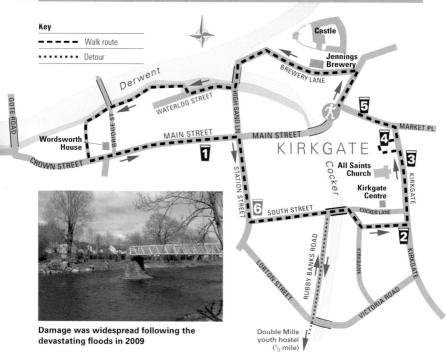

Key

- - - - - Walk route
· · · · · · · Detour

Derwent

WATERLOO STREET

HIGH SAND LN

GOTE ROAD

BRIDGE ST

MAIN STREET

CROWN STREET

Wordsworth House

Castle

Jennings Brewery

BREWERY LANE

MARKET PL.

5

4

3

MAIN STREET

KIRKGATE

Cocker

All Saints Church

Kirkgate Centre

STATION STREET

6

SOUTH STREET

COCKER LANE

KIRKGATE

KIRKBANK

KIRKGATE

2

1

LORTON STREET

RUBY BANKS ROAD

VICTORIA ROAD

Damage was widespread following the devastating floods in 2009

Double Mills youth hostel (¹/₂ mile)

The best place to start is in the Castle-gate, at the junction with the Market Place, just east of the river bridge. The town received its Market Charter in 1221. There was a moot hall in the middle of the wide roadway here at the foot of the Kirkgate, but it was demolished around 1830.

Walk up the handsome and narrow Castlegate, lined with tall buildings, and take the left turn into Brewery Lane, walking down towards the Castle Brewery. Incidentally the castle, which dates back to Norman times, is not open to the public as a rule. It's partly a ruin and partly a private residence. Jennings Brewery moved to Cockermouth in 1874 having been established in the village of Lorton earlier in the century. There's no longer a Jennings family connection, but at least we still have the beers. For brewery tours see www. jenningsbrewery.co.uk/tours or call 0845 129 7190.

Jennings Brewery entrance

Beyond the brewery you reach the Derwent by its confluence with the Cocker. This was formerly an industrial area with tanneries and metalworking factories in addition to the brewery – but is now a quiet spot with a footbridge over the Cocker. Cross this and take first right into Waterloo Street. Although the factories have gone the old Wharton's mill on the left is unmistakable, and once made linen. In 200 yards or so turn back down to the river by a modern block of flats on the site of another old mill, this once was the Graves woollen mill. Go under the footbridge, and turn left up the lane. Note just before you reach the main road, a plaque commemorating Fearon Fallows, who was born in a cottage here, and went on to become Astronomer Royal.

Turn left here into Crown Street which soon becomes the Main Street. Immediately on the left is Wordsworth House, a mid 18th-century Georgian house and the birthplace

LEFT: **Inside the Swan Inn, a rare outlet for Jennings Dark Mild** RIGHT: **The Bitter End pub**

of the great poet. It's now owned by the National Trust and is open to the public. Next door is the Printing House Museum. Continue along the street and detour briefly down Cockton's Yard, one of what was once many yards developed in the industrial revolution – the simple yet handsome workers' cottages and weaving workshops, built in what was once the burgage plot (garden) of the large house fronting the street, have been restored with a grant from English Heritage. Cross the road here (the fine marble statue in the centre of the street is Richard Southwell Bourke, sixth earl of Mayo, and MP for Cockermouth between 1857-68 who was then elevated to Viceroy and Governor-General of India before being assassinated in 1872, whilst visiting the Andaman Islands). Across the street here is the **Bush Hotel 1** which was shut for around six months after the floods but should by now be once again serving a wide range of Jennings beers. It needed some significant work after the floods but they haven't otherwise messed around with this historic low-beamed two-room pub, the front room being the more traditional in feel, with an open fire. Expect this *Good Beer Guide* regular to be busy in the evenings especially at weekends. Lunchtime food is available.

Continue past the statue and turn right into Station Street, then take the first left into South Street (where you may well wish to call in at the **Tithe Barn 6** with its attractive stained glass and Jennings beers) and walk along to the river. This was another area very badly affected by flooding. The new flats on the riverside here have been converted from an old hat factory: this was another important local industry of one time and made good use of rabbit skins handed over by local farmers. If you have time on your hands it makes a pleasant diversion to follow the riverside upstream here to the former 17th-century watermill of Double Mills (now a youth hostel), a walk of about half a mile in each direction – simply keep close to the river and you can't go wrong.

Back at the end of South Street, cross the footbridge and start up Cocker Lane ahead, taking the steps on the right after a few yards which lead you up Kirk Bank to a former bleaching ground which is now one of the best viewpoints over the town. There is a Civic Trust interpretive panel to help you with all the sights. Worth looking out for in particular is the castle just to the right of the brewery, and a little further away to the left at Papcastle, the site of an old Roman Fort. From Kirk Bank continue along Mackreth Row which brings you conveniently out onto Kirkgate right next to the **Swan Inn 2**. An excellent traditional pub, it's one of the oldest and most unspoilt remaining in the town with plenty of character despite having been partially opened out. To the left as you enter is the traditional floorboarded bar with a solid fuel range whilst to the right a lounge and best room lie at a slightly lower level. This Jennings house is a rare outlet for the brewery's excellent Dark Mild Ale.

Walking downhill from the Swan brings you into the Georgian square off Kirkgate lined with handsome 18th-century houses. If the cobbled square is not completely littered with cars you may be able to find the outline of a stag in the stones towards the southern end. As you reach

the foot of the square you'll see the sign for next pub on the right hand side of the street: the **Bitter End** 3 is a well-known drinkers' landmark even though it's no longer a brew-pub – the brewery having moved to an industrial estate in town. The characterful interior has three main areas: a wood-floored front bar with two rear rooms. The pub still showcases the interesting Bitter End brews, as well as some guests including Jennings. Dining is a major focus here as well, and even the name is a clever play on words for a short distance downhill, by the Kirkgate Centre arts and entertainment venue, runs the Bitter Beck, a small stream which got its name from the tannery effluent which once polluted it.

Across the street from the Bitter End an alleyway leads into the precincts of All Saints Church; built in 1852, it's the fourth church recorded on this site. From the sloping ground below the church or at the bottom of Kirkgate if you walk straight down the road, you'll come to the rear of **1761** 4, a recently opened bar with a contemporary ambience inside. Currently only open from the late afternoon (2pm weekends) the attraction for

the drinker is the range of ales: a rare outlet for Yates Bitter, as well as several changing guest beers, with local Cumbrian brews prominent.

The front of 1761 gives on to the top of the Market Place and walking to the left brings you back down to the start of the route by the junction with Castlegate. But on the right and frankly unmissable with its fairly lurid external paint job, is the **Castle Bar** 5 . This is very much the new kid on the block as far as cask ales are concerned: a recent makeover has given this former Matthew Brown house a very contemporary and smart new image. The very interesting interior has several interconnected rooms leading off a floorboarded front bar: and for once here the beams look genuinely old. It's a sign of the revival of cask beer that pubs like this although aimed at a young set are offering a range of interesting beers and here the choice is as good as anywhere in town with three changing guests alongside Jennings Bitter. Expect lots of comfy sofas as well as the vertical drinking space. There's a good food menu so you can wait until this last pub to eat if that suits your plans. To get to the bus stop simply return to Castlegate at the foot of the road and turn left and walk back over the river towards the Mayo statue.

PUB INFORMATION

1 Bush Hotel
Main Street, Cockermouth,
CA13 9JS
01900 822064
Opening Hours: 11-midnight
(11 Sun)

2 Swan Inn
52-56 Kirkgate, Cockermouth,
CA13 9PH
01900 822425
Opening Hours: 6-11.30
(midnight Fri); 11-midnight Sat;
12-11 Sun

3 Bitter End
15 Kirkgate, Cockermoth, CA13 9PJ
01900 828993
www.bitterend.co.uk
Opening Hours:
12-2.30 & 6-11.00;
12-midnight
Fri-Sat

4 1761
1 Market Place, Cockermouth,
CA13 9NG
01900 829282
www.bar1761.co.uk
Opening Hours: 4.30-11;
12-11.30 Sat; 4.30-11.30 Sun

5 Castle Bar
14 Market Place, Cockermouth,
CA13 9NQ
01900 829904
Opening Hours: 4.30-11;
12-midnight Fri & Sat;
12-10.30 Sun

Try also:

6 Tithe Barn
41 Station Street, Cockermouth,
CA13 9QW
01900 822179
www.tithebarncockermouth.co.uk
Opening Hours: 11-midnight;
12-11 Sun; closed Mon

The Bitter End

CAMPAIGN FOR REAL ALE
WEST CUMBRIA
AWARD
WINNING PUB
With
Own Micro Brewery
(On View Inside)
Quality Bar Meals
Available
Lunchtime 12.00-2.00 Evenings 6.00-8.30
Sundays 12.00-2.00 & 6.00-8.30

Loweswater & Crummock

WALK INFORMATION

Start/ Finish: Scalehill bridge (🔍 149215)

Access: Summer bus 77/77A from Keswick

Distance: 5 miles (8km) for full round. 2.6 km (4km) for short round

OS map: OS Explorer OL4

Key attractions: Award-winning pub; lakeshore walking

The pubs: Kirkstile Inn, Loweswater

A varied round in the quieter but well-loved north-western corner of the national park, skirting the northern end of peaceful Crummock Water and the lower shoulder of Mellbreak, with some sections of woodland to vary the scenery. The real draw for the dedicated pub hound is a visit to the multi-award winning Kirkstile Inn, the 'tap' for the Cumbrian Legendary Ales brewery. As is common in this book, there is a shorter option, which will halve the total distance. Public transport is sparse here, so plan carefully if you're relying on the 77 bus to get you home; a timely point at which to point out that the Kirkstile Inn offers accommodation. Navigation needs a little care on some sections of the full circuit, but it would be difficult to get completely lost. Also, if it's been very wet, some sections of the route near Crummock Water are prone to flooding so ensure you're adequately shod and clad if you attempt the route during or after heavy rain.

Crummock Water

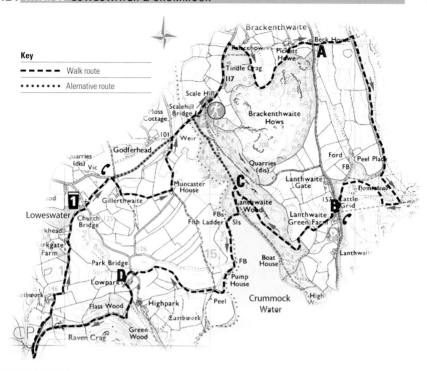

Key
- - - - Walk route
• • • • • Alernative route

The remote Lowpark Cottage near Flass Wood

Start at the car park by Scalehill Bridge (or if arriving by route 77/77A bus alight at Beck House – see point A, below).

If you want to follow the shorter loop, missing out the Whiteside crags section it will save at least an hour on the round. Take the good path through the woods towards the lake, keeping right where the path branches, to pick up the main route below at point C.

If following the longer route, walk up the lane away from the river bridge (taking care since there is no footpath) until you join a wood on the right hand-side. It's easiest to walk about 100 yards past the footpath sign through the wood to a gate to with a National Trust sign. Enter the woodland here and take the good stony path through the woodland, but fork left towards the far corner of the wood in about five minutes where a narrow path goes to a step stone stile over a wall. Then follow the track towards the farm across to your left. Here go through the gate and over the brow of the hill to join the B5289 road, and the bus route, at Beck House.

Directly opposite, a footpath crosses the stream (A, 157220). Be aware that this foot-bridge opposite Beck House was destroyed in the 2009 floods. If it is still missing it's not an un-pleasant alternative simply to turn right at Beck House and follow the road southwards for about two thirds of a mile, past the first bridleway on the right and the buildings at Lanthwaite Gate, to rejoin the route at the footpath by Lanthwaite Green Farm and point B.

If the bridge is passable, cross the river and follow the wall for about 250 yards before joining a path at the top of the field which runs along the top wall under the crags. Turn right and follow this. When the wall curves away right in about half a mile bear slightly left downhill towards the bracken to cross the little beck by a footbridge, then follow the bank of the river downhill. This is an area where enormous devastation was caused by the recent floods, and this tiny stream was transformed into a real torrent: the results can be seen around you here, including the loss of the lower footbridge.

Swing away from the stream as it curves to the right, to meet a wall and a farm track; bear left and follow it for the very short walk across to the road at Lanthwaite Green Farm (B,  159208). Cross the road and take the path towards the trees.

One of the few remaining places to see the red squirrel

When you go through the gate into the woodland the track curves around (left first) in a tight arc to become a wider forest track leading you in a north-westerly direction above the northern end of Crummock Water, downhill through the trees of Lanthwaite Wood. When you meet another track – the one coming from the car park at the start of the walk (C, 152211) – double back by turning sharply left and down to the lake shore where there is a thoughtfully placed seat.

Cross over the incipient River Cocker on two robust footbridges, then follow the path right on the lake shore towards the pump house close by. Cross another footbridge by the pump house and then head inland for about 250 yards to the visible footbridge. Don't cross this but turn left for another 150 yards and right on the walkboards just before the gate. Pick up the path across the marshy section here – it curves gently

The route skirts the very edge of Crummock Water – literally!

Kirkstile Inn

towards the stream you recently crossed and for the last section is confined pleasantly by a wall and some open woodland to join the little lane at Lowpark (D,  145204).

This is a very quiet spot nestling peacefully under the northern end of Mellbreak towards whose steep crags you turn shortly, having found the bridleway sign just 20 yards down the lane. Follow this past the house and up into Flass Wood with Highpark House just a few yards off to your left. The bridleway turns sharply right near the top of the woodland and contours along the foot of Mellbreak with a wall on your right. In sunshine this stretch is one of the high points of the walk.

Join the bridleway running north–south in 600 yards (or take a short cut through the clearing to the gate below before that) and simply follow the track downhill past Kirkgate Farm to the tiny hamlet of Loweswater where opposite the little chapel lies the **Kirkstile Inn 1**.

In a photogenic setting this classic Lakeland inn has attracted plenty of superlatives, and a fistful of local CAMRA awards. The welcoming bar, which is frequently busy, is run efficiently, and offers an extensive beer menu from the stable of Cumbrian Legendary Ales. This was once the Loweswater brewery, based here at the

Kirkstile Inn, but although still owned by the licensee the brewery has been moved out. You won't taste any great difference in the quality of the excellent ales though. There are several drinking and eating areas in the extended and opened-out bar which retains character and an attractive open fire. The lined pint glasses are another welcome sight in an area where short measure is all too common. There's even a rare shove ha'penny board which flummoxed a group of younger visitors (who clearly had never seen one before) on my last visit. If the weather's good there's a pleasant garden at the rear of the pub which is about as peaceful a place to consume your pint as you could wish for.

To return to the start, walk up the lane which goes to the right of the church as you face it, joining the main road at near Gillerthwaite. It's either half a mile along the road back to Scale Hill, or time permitting, walk down the farm track to Gillerthwaite (150 yards) and take the footpath on the left just beyond the buildings across to Muncaster House close by. Then bear left again on the lane to rejoin the main road much closer to the car park.

PUB INFORMATION

1 Kirkstile Inn
Loweswater, CA13 0RU
01900 85219
www.kirkstile.com
Opening Hours: 10-11 (10.30 Sun)

> LINK Walk 20, Buttermere round, via summer bus 77 from stop at Beck House (4 miles).

Cumberland Group – the East

The peaceful village of Caldbeck

Bampton & Haweswater

WALK INFORMATION

Start/Finish: Bampton Bridge (515182)

Access: Very limited by public transport. Penrith station (8 miles); Shap (4 miles)

Distance: 6.2 miles (10km)

OS map: OS Explorer OL5

Key attractions: Haweswater reservoir; *Withnail and I* film locations

The pubs: Mardale Inn, Bampton; Crown & Mitre, Bampton Grange. Try also: Greyhound, Shap (4 miles)

The upper end of Haweswater

By the standards of the walks in this book, this circuit takes you into some fairly wild and remote country, albeit only briefly. These far eastern fells of Lakeland surrounding the hidden Haweswater reservoir (see box) are relatively unfrequented, and you may have the open fell section to yourself. Views are extensive, and include the reservoir itself, although the route stays high above the water. The route ascends to as high as around 1,800 feet, one of the highest points on any walk in this book. In good weather the navigation is fairly straightforward, but unless you're an experienced hill walker, I would advise against attempting this route in mist. A map and compass should be carried, and if the weather closes in whilst in the vicinity of Low Kop, it's safe if steep to take a bearing off the fell and down to the lake. Bampton village itself is clustered around the bridge over Howes Beck, and has an attractive architectural and historic character. Both pubs on this route offer food and accommodation.

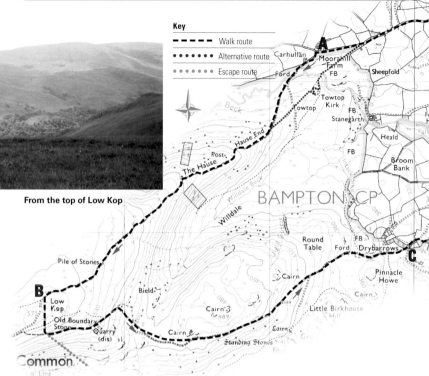

Key

- - - - Walk route
•••••• Alternative route
•••••• Escape route

From the top of Low Kop

From the centre of Bampton on the bridge, start by walking up the road leading northwards towards Penrith, (bear left facing the shop) and in a hundred yards or so, by the telephone box (used in cult 80's film *Withnail and I*) take the unfenced road to the left, over the cattle grid, which immediately climbs very steeply through an attractive area of bracken and gorse. Keep on the tarred road as it twists and climbs steadily uphill, passing the farm buildings of Hullockhowe in about half a mile, and continue towards the end of the road at Moorahill Farm (A, ⊕ 494182).

Across to your left you'll see a distinct pointed nose of a ridge leading up into the fells, and from the farm a fingerboard points out a path along the left-hand side of the wall down to the beck which it crosses and then climbs to gain the ridge. Warning: in wet weather or when the stream is high it may be too difficult to cross the beck without shipping water at this point. Help is at hand: a well-hidden stone clapper bridge crosses the beck a short distance downstream, immediately below the farm, and indeed a good track leads straight down to this bridge from the road about

150 yards before you reach the farm (see map).

Either way you should shortly be on the clear track which climbs the spur onto the rounded ridge ahead of you. Climb steadily, taking your time as the ascent is sustained if not overly steep; there should be good views opening up across the Pennines, with Cross Fell prominent, but also the Lowther valley, and the lime works near Shap. This section is the remotest on the walk with the lonely valleys running up towards the High Street ridge and Loadpot Hill ahead. We are heading for Low Kop, an undistinguished top which is really little more than a plateau, where the ascent levels out just over a mile after gaining the ridge.

The grassy path which has served us so well on the ascent continues beyond Low Kop to the equally undistinguished High Kop: so at the point (B, ⊕ 475166) where the track levels off and threatens to descend slightly, with a clear view ahead towards the continuing ridge and the skyline beyond, bear left across the grass, heading due south, to gain the admittedly rather unexciting top of Low Kop. Once you can see in all directions, you know you're on the summit! If you continue

walking on the same bearing a short while longer, starting downhill now, the lake, Haweswater, very quickly comes into view below you. Walk a short way down the fairly steep slope until you meet a very clear grassy track crossing at right angles, contouring along the hill.

If the weather has closed in and the priority is to descend off the hill quickly, it's safe although very steep to continue more less straight ahead into the valley below you, but don't expect a clear path – the green track shown on the Ordnance Survey map is misleading in this respect – but if you do end up taking this route down you should be able to reach the footbridge across the stream and beyond it the lake shore where you'll pick up a much better path and with the aid of your map this will eventually return you to the village.

If the weather is fine, join the track turning left and just let the path guide you downhill towards the unnamed summit ahead of you, marked with a clear cairn. Simply keep on the prominent path, which skirts the aforementioned summit, keeping it on your left with a series of smaller knolls across on your right. Cross the slightly boggy area which is shown on the map before reaching Upper Drybarrows farm, and a gate in the wall by the right-hand end of a line of trees (C, ⊙ 169500). Disregard the illegally placed

HAWESWATER RESERVOIR

The Mardale valley was flooded by Manchester Corporation in the mid 1930s after a 1929 Act of Parliament giving permission caused a furore: the valley was regarded as one of the most attractive in the region. There was originally a smaller Haweswater, but the project raised the water level by almost 100 feet and meant the loss of two villages, Measand and Mardale Green, as well as an ancient inn, the Dun Bull, and Mardale church – whose stone was later incorporated in the dam. Technological anoraks may know that this was the world's first hollow buttress dam, and when full the reservoir can hold 18.5 billion gallons of water. Manchester Corporation built a new road along the eastern side of the lake and the Haweswater Hotel was built to replace the old Dun Bull. The ghosts of the old villages can partially be seen when the reservoir is very low.

The view shortly after setting off down from Low Kop

LEFT: **The Crown & Mitre at Bampton Grange** RIGHT: **Mardale Inn, Bampton**

diversion sign by the gate: the right of way goes through the gate and farmyard here.

Once round the house bear towards the wall on the right (disregard the Land Rover track bearing off to the left), through an opening in the wall (or a stone stile nearby) and then make for the first of four ladder stiles taking you through the fields. Once over the fourth of these, keep straight ahead across the knoll in front and down to an exit stile by a fingerpost onto a small lane.

About 50 yards down the lane another signed post ('Bampton') takes you left onto another path. Take the right-hand of the two gates on offer ahead, and follow a very indistinct track veering slowly away from the wall on your left, to cross another ladder stile. Beyond, the land falls away more steeply and you're looking into the Lowther valley with Brampton Grange visible. Navigation is simple now: aim for the building directly ahead of you in the bottom corner of the field, and simply follow ahead through the metal gate, keeping the wood and wire fence on your left, (don't go through the gate into the left-hand field) until this line disgorges you onto the lane at the bottom, where simply turn left and a hundred yards along is the **Mardale Inn** 🚩 .

Set in a terrace of old cottages in this quiet village,

the inn, formerly called St Patrick's Well, has been given a distinctive and significant internal reworking by its new owners, which belies the traditional façade. Nonetheless it's been done tastefully although perhaps the sharp lines of the wooden tables and chairs and the stone floor lack a degree of comfortable informality. There are up to four changing beers available, sometimes including those unusual for the area. The place takes its food seriously and offers a wide range of plates, with an emphasis on local sourcing, and also offers accommodation.

If it's open (see times), it's well worth the short walk down to the Crown & Mitre. From the Mardale Inn, return to the centre of the village a few yards below, and it's only about a quarter of a mile along the lane to the right before you reach the sister settlement of Brampton Grange. Turn left over the bridge and opposite St Patrick's church is the **Crown & Mitre** 🚩 . This smart village pub-cum-hotel has a lively public bar and three ales on offer: Black Sheep Bitter, one from Tirril brewery and a rotating guest, again with food and accommodation.

If you're leaving the area via Shap, the **Greyhound** (off map) at the far south of this straggly settlement strung out along the A6 offers a range of beers and good value food.

PUB INFORMATION

1 **Mardale Inn**
Bampton, CA10 2RQ
01931 713244
www.mardaleinn.co.uk
Opening Hours: 11-11 (10.30 Sun)

2 **Crown & Mitre**
Bampton Grange, CA10 2QR
01931 713225
www.crownandmitre.com
Opening Hours: 6 (12 Sat)-11 winter; 6-midnight summer; 5-10.30 Sun winter; 2-midnight Sun summer

TRY ALSO:

Greyhound
Main Street, Shap, CA10 3PW
01931 716474
www.greyhoundshap.co.uk
Opening Hours: 11-11

A circuit from Caldbeck via Hesket Newmarket

WALK INFORMATION

Start/Finish: Caldbeck village (or Hesket Newmarket)

Access: Caldbeck Rambler bus service 73/73A runs Saturdays, some Sundays and daily in school summer holidays. See www.keswick. org/getting_about.asp; and don't miss the last bus home!

Distance: 6 miles (9.5km)

OS map: OS Explorer OL5

Key attractions: Old Crown, Hesket Newmarket; Back o' Skiddaw

The pubs: Old Crown, Hesket Newmarket; Oddfellows Arms, Caldbeck

The village green at Caldbeck

Splendid though the scenery in this secluded corner of Lakeland is, this walk is very much a case of the tail wagging the dog, for no book of pub walks in the Lakes is complete without reference to the remarkable Old Crown at Hesket Newmarket, a community-run pub with its own brewery attached. It's a great example of the pub at the hub of a rural community. Add to this Caldbeck – a charming village which was once the centre of an extensive mining area but is now a tranquil backwater with some fine buildings, a working mill and its own vibrant pub – and we have all the ingredients for a top day out. Weather permitting you'll also enjoy fine views of the northern side of the big whaleback of Skiddaw, one of Lakeland's four + 3,000 foot mountains. The going is moderate and navigation should pose no real problems.

Key

- – – – Walk route
- •••••• Alternative route

A quiet backwater in Caldbeck

Caldbeck is the natural starting point for this walk. It's a sizeable village and has some attractive buildings as well as a pleasant village green and pond, and two excellent cafés. Caldbeck is named after the river Cold Beck, which provided water power for industry in the 17th and 18th centuries. Mills producing flour, wool, bobbins and paper, along with a brewery, all used the river and many of these old buildings still exist in the village. It's also possible to start the walk at Hesket Newmarket, particularly if you want to end up there in the evening too take full advantage of the Old Crown Inn.

In Caldbeck make your way to the churchyard of St Kentigern's Church. At the north-east corner of the churchyard, accessible down the lane from the main road, is the Watermill Café, part of Priests Mill, which occupies an enviable spot by the river. A morning coffee in the sunny garden is guaranteed to get the walk off to a good start.

Follow the river on a narrow path adjacent the churchyard and cross the footbridge to join the lane on the north bank of the stream, turning left past some attractive cottages to the road junction. There are some very pretty and colourful cottages across the river to your left, leading up to the Oddfellows Arms and the Old Smithy tearoom/gift shop; but our route climbs the short hill to the right and bears first left by idyllic village pond at the top of the brae, doubling back along a quieter lane.

Straight ahead and looking like a private entry is a gate (look for the waymark sign on the wall). This is the path, which soon regains the riverside just before the Howk, a limestone gorge containing waterfalls and the picturesque ruins of the old bobbin mill. The path climbs steeply through the gorge. Cross by the footbridge to the gate on the other side of the river and then keep close to the wall on your left as the right of way climbs up to meet the road. The northern fringes of the Lakeland hills dominate the view, with High Pike prominent, and it's towards these fells that the next stage of the walk leads. Turn left back towards the village for a few yards before taking the right turn into a quiet lane lined with cottages. Just as the houses come to an end, the lane crosses a small beck and offers three diverging routes. Take the central option ('no-through road' sign) and simply follow this tarred lane for the best part of a mile until it peters out in the little farming hamlet of Nether Row. You're unlikely to meet any traffic on this road.

The Old Crown at Hesket Newmarket

At Nether Row head round to the left of the prominent white house, ignoring the signed footpath to Potts Gill, and then follow a signed path off to the left over a small beck and a stile, heading into some fields between two belts of trees in the middle distance. The right of way is unclear on the ground, but head for the top of the right-hand tree belt, and then let the wall lead you up to the top right-hand corner of the field where you cross the prominent ladder stile into the open country beyond (A, ⊙ 329376).

THE OLD CROWN – A PUB AT THE HUB OF THE VILLAGE

The Hesket Newmarket Brewery Co-operative was born in 2000 after locals rejected an investor buyout of the successful micro-brewery when the owners retired. It became apparent that many investors were more interested in the resale value of the brewery land, rather than the brewery itself or the economic fortunes of the wider community. Instead, local people came up with the idea of forming a brewery co-operative, a community enterprise run on democratic principles through which members who lived locally or had local connections could own equal shares. The business is a social enterprise which nurtures local connections – for example, spent grains from the brewing process are sent to a farmer who grows organic produce and rears organic cattle. The co-operative also assists by ploughing shares of the profits into local community projects.

After the community bought the brewery, the next stage came when 120 members formed a

The micro brewery at the Old Crown

further community co-op to buy the Old Crown pub from retiring landlord Kim Matthews. Regulars at the Cumbrian village pub feared their local might close down or fall into the hands of a big brewery chain after it went up for sale so they formed the co-op to safeguard the Old Crown's future as a community business. Local people recognised that if the pub closed, that would also threaten the local post office, shop and bed & breakfast. Ownership by the community co-op will help preserve not only the independence and unique character of the pub, but will also allow the village to retain its sense of community and ensure it remains a vibrant place to live. Julian Ross, who led the ownership bid, says: "People say they don't care about the returns: they want to preserve something that's important for the community. This is a cosy, friendly pub, which you can go into whether you're wearing your wellies, walking boots, or a suit, and you won't come out without speaking to someone."

Oddfellows Arms

Keep the wall on your immediate left. This area may be a bit boggy in wet weather, but you're only this side of the wall for about 150 yards, before turning left through the gate into the farmyard at Hudscales. Now excellent views spread out before you across the agricultural country towards the Solway Firth. Walk downhill, and where the farm track swings left by two metal gates, an un-signed right of way leads through the right-hand gate and heads downhill (keep the wall, and later a fence, on your left) towards the wind turbine ahead of you. Soon, Hesket Newmarket comes into view below you. Most of the fields have a stile, and following this line, you should pick up the route down to the village. In the lowest field you keep the wire fence close on your right, entering the lane into the village through a gap in railings by a double gabled house.

Hesket Newmarket is a charming village with a linear village green, lined with attractive houses. Star of the show of course is the **Old Crown** halfway down on the right.

The Old Crown is deservedly well-known among beer drinkers for its fine locally-brewed beers and for being the first British example of a community owned pub (see box). In addition it's a handsome three-roomed pub offering a friendly welcome and all the attributes that make the pub a great social institution. The Old Crown offers half a dozen of its own beers on handpump, in a traditional bar with simple dining room beyond, and a games room with juke box at the other end is popular in the evenings with the local youngsters – and why not? Food here is highly recommended but such is the popularity of the place that advance booking is recommended if you are intend-ing to eat here in the evening. The food service does not de-tract from the key focus of the pub: to offer a warm welcome to drinkers and serve them an excellent pint. Doris, the cheery nonogenerian smiling at you from the pump clips, by the way, was the mother-in-law of an earlier landlord. Some proper old-fashioned urinals (for those of us who appreciate

that sort of thing) complete the picture.

The signed path back to Caldbeck is directly across the road and the green. The first half a mile is a delightful downhill stroll, firstly down towards the little River Caldew, through a couple of small copses and then into more open meadow keeping the river on your right. You end up on a narrow neck where the Caldew on your right is a matter of yards from the larger Cald Beck on your left, crossing the latter on the footbridge. It's a worth-while short detour to carry on to the 'watersmeet' by walking down the wooded promontory for a couple of hundred yards.

A short but stiff ascent of the northern bank of the Cald Beck brings you to up first to a stile, then left to a gate on the Cumbria Way path, which you simply follow through the woods (with glimpses of the fells through the trees) and downhill again to rejoin the river for the last stretch into Caldbeck. You'll recognise the Watermill Café and just through the gate, the church tower of St Kentigerns comes into view once more. This time cross the narrow footbridge and head up to the road at the top of the churchyard, where turn right and you'll see the village pub, the **Oddfellows Arms**.

This village local is a Jennings house serving their Bitter and Cumberland Ale, with a seasonal guest from the brewery's range. The separate split-level dining room serves food (including an *a-la-carte* menu) both lunchtimes and evenings; and usefully, given the relative remoteness of this area, offers accommodation.

PUB INFORMATION

1 **Old Crown**
Hesket Newmarket, CA7 8JG
016974 78288
www.theoldcrownpub.co.uk
Opening Hours: 12-3 Fri-Sun only, 5.30-11 (10.30 Sun)

2 **Oddfellows Arms**
Caldbeck, Wigton, CA7 8EA
01697 478227
www.oddfellows-caldbeck.co.uk
Opening Hours: 12-3 (not Mon-Thu), 7 (6 Fri & Sat)-11; 12-10.30 Sun

Grasmere to Ambleside via Rydal

WALK INFORMATION

Start: Grasmere village

Finish: Wateredge Inn, Ambleside

Access: Bus 555 connects with the railway at Windermere, and runs frequently along the A591, connecting sections of the route

Distance: 7 miles (11.25km)

OS map: OS Explorer OL7

Key attractions: Dove Cottage, Grasmere; Rydal Hall; White Moss Common and viewpoint; Loughrigg Terrace viewpoint and Loughrigg Fell

The pubs: Badger Bar (Rothay Hotel), Rydal; Golden Rule, Queen's Hotel, Wateredge Inn, all Ambleside. Try also: Tweedies Bar, Grasmere

A short walk along the line of the main north–south route through the Eastern Lakes, well-punctuated with good views, plenty of water and plenty of beer. Culture vultures will enjoy Grasmere with its Wordsworth connections, in particular Dove Cottage his home; whilst more energetic fellwalkers can take in Loughrigg Fell which has excellent all-round views despite its relatively modest height. There are good cafés both at Dove Cottage close to the start of the walk and at Rydal Hall, halfway along. Ambleside itself offers the visitor a good choice of beers; whilst the excellent Tweedies Bar in Grasmere is an obvious place to return to if you're staying in that village; in which case the frequent 555 bus will take you almost to the door once you've finished in Ambleside.

Grasmere from Loughrigg Terrace

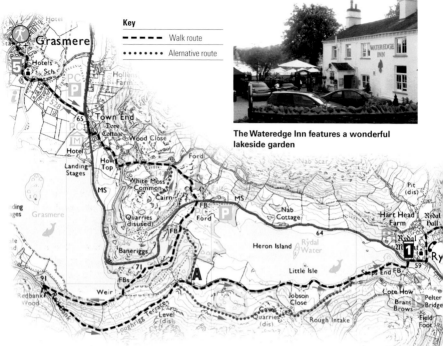

Key
- - - - Walk route
••••••• Alernative route

The Wateredge Inn features a wonderful lakeside garden

From Grasmere village, walk down towards the church on the B5287 road, taking note of the Dale Lodge Hotel on Red Bank Road off to the right, which houses **Tweedies Bar 5** which is well worth returning to after your walk. Provided you promise to leave and do the walk afterwards, you're even allowed a quick sortie before you get going! With seven handpumps and a mouthwatering variety of changing beers, mainly from Cumbria and Scotland, this comfortable stone-flagged bar is a great find for the discerning ale taster. Food here too is highly rated, and in the view of most patrons, worth the premium in price you expect to pay in a tourist destination like Grasmere.

Carrying on to the main road junction at Town End, almost directly opposite is Wordsworth's Dove Cottage and the Wordsworth Museum. The cottage, which allegedly was once a pub named the Dove & Olive, is a quaint building well worth a visit. There's also a small cafeteria which you may wish to make use of.

Picking up the walk, take the minor road which runs behind the museum uphill and away from the busy A591 road. At How Top in about 300

yards where the lane veers to the right, take a bridleway which continues ahead signed as the 'coffin road' to Rydal. Before the days of tarred roads coffin roads were used to carry the dead to the nearest consecrated ground. Climb up the lane onto the pleasantly wooded promontory of White Moss Common. You just have time to become jealous of the massive houses tucked in behind the rhododendrons before reaching a small but mature pond where there's a good bridleway dropping off to your right. Before descending here you may wish to take the short detour (and it is short) to the summit of White Moss Common off to the right: there is a seat *en route*, and at the top, a worthwhile view out across Rydal Water below you.

The bridleway leads quickly down to the main road by a small car park well-hidden in the trees. Cross carefully and, passing the public toilet pavilion, walk down to the footbridge over a stream which runs the short distance between Rydal Water and Grasmere. If you're pushed for time you could cut twenty minutes off the walk by crossing here and taking the short but steep uphill path through the trees to join the main route at (A,

347060); but you'd miss Loughrigg Terrace, one of the highlights of the walk, so I don't recommend it unless *in extremis*!

Follow the river downstream to the next bridge in about 400 yards and, crossing here, you emerge close to the southern end of Grasmere lake. The two lakes were left behind after the last ice age when a glacier running down from the north into what is now Windermere encountered the tough rock at White Moss and left two the lakes in the deepened troughs on either side.

Walk along the shore of the lake and through the gate at the far end into the trees. Now take the higher (left-hand) path which climbs (but not too steeply) through the trees to join the little road over to Elterwater. Almost immediately double back sharply on another path which climbs, more steeply this time, to reach a junction of routes at the National Trust's Loughrigg estate. Walk through the gate and onto the delightful Loughrigg Terrace which offers wonderful open views across Grasmere lake towards the village. There are plenty of seats to assist your enjoyment of the view.

Now follow the well-trodden

RYDAL HALL

Rydal Hall, now a Christian community offering accommodation from camping and bunkhouse to full board, was sold to the Diocese of Carlisle in the 1960s having previously been a private estate. The attractive hall is set in over 30 acres of gardens and surrounded by a much larger estate. The gardens were designed by landscape architect Thomas Mawson in 1910 with herbaceous borders and lawns and a restored summerhouse overlooking the Rydal Falls popularised by Wordsworth. The old walled kitchen garden houses an orchard planted with, among other things, 30 varieties of apples. Of more practical interest to us is the shop, open 10-5 daily.

path to the end of the Terrace and then down a short steep section (joining the short-cut path emerging through a gap in the wall on your left); (A, 347060); and along a lower path close to the shore of Rydal Water. A higher path running off to the right hereabouts is an alternative which rejoins the main route at the far end of the lake.

Towards the end of the charming lake the path enters a wooded area and, keeping close to the shore, you'll arrive at a bridge over the emerging River Rothay which takes you straight onto the main road, but importantly, right opposite the Rothay Hotel and the welcoming **Badger Bar 1** . This attractive little roadside bar retains a good deal of character, and has a compact but irregular layout, with both a small floorboard area around the servery and a very comfortable lounge (the latter with carved wooden wall panelling and a large fireplace). Importantly there are hand-pumps dispensing a changing range of up to five ales, with a strong emphasis on local brews. Food

Evening alongside Rydal Water

is served lunchtimes until 2.30, evenings until 8.30 (later at weekends). Nearby is Rydal Mount, the final home of William Wordsworth.

Leaving the hotel turn left and at the church, left again and walk up the steep access lane to Rydal Hall which is now a residential centre (see box). Turn into the Hall grounds by the tea room sign, where we rejoin the coffin road, and weave your way through the outbuildings of the hall itself within which there's a well-regarded café if you feel like refreshments of a non-alcoholic kind.

The path crosses the Rydal Beck and continues through the grounds of the Hall and the next half a mile offers a pleasant stroll though more formal parkland with fine views across to Loughrigg Fell across to your right. Emerge onto the main road by the old lodge, and although there's a bus stop there (which might tempt you if a bus is imminent) the roadside walk, whilst noisy, is not so long. Bear left for Ambleside and in half a mile you're in the centre of town with all the fleshpots the place has to offer. Shortly after passing the quaint but frankly over-rated Bridge House on the right at the outskirts of town, bear left at the mini roundabout ('Kirkstile') and walk fifty yards steeply uphill on Smithy Brow to the **Golden Rule 2**.

When it was a Hartley's house this traditional pub was the discerning drinker's first port of call in Ambleside: a multi-roomed interior with no piped music or any other modern distractions like food. Robinson's have altered the place little, although

In the Queen's Hotel, Ambleside

depending on your taste you may have views about the changed beer menu. It's still very much worth a visit though, and offers six beers from the Robinson's stable on handpump. There's a small yard/garden at the rear.

Leave the pub and bear right onto North Road, passing the *Unicorn* on the way downhill (if you're looking for additional pubs this is one worth trying) to reach the main road again close to the Sportsmans Inn and the **Queen's Hotel 3**. This food-oriented bar makes up for what it lacks in pubbiness by offering Ambleside's widest range of beers: Jennings and Yates's bitter with up to four rotating guests, once again with an emphasis upon Cumbrian brewers. I wouldn't bother with the downstairs cellar bar unless you're very young and/or addicted to TV and pool.

I'd recommend bussing it the mile southwards down Lake Road to Waterhead where at the junction by the Waterhead Hotel and the northern end of Lake Windermere, double sharply back on the lower road the A5075 for 150 yards to the **Wateredge Inn 4**, right, as the name suggests, on the lake shore, with its own waterside garden. Expect the excellent Coniston Bluebird plus up to two changing guests. It isn't cheap, but it's worth the premium to drink in the lovely view, and you can eat here too: recommended if the weather's fine. The bus stop for Ambleside town centre and Grasmere is back on the main road 50 yards north of the junction.

PUB INFORMATION

1 Badger Bar
(Glen Rothay Hotel)
Rydal, LA22 9LR
015394 34500
www.theglenrothay.co.uk
Opening Hours: 11-11 (10.30 Sun)

2 Golden Rule
Smithy Brow, Ambleside,
LA22 9AS
015394 32257
Opening Hours: 11 (12 Sun)-
midnight

3 Queen's Hotel
Market Place, Ambleside, LA22 9BU
015394 32206
www.queenshotelambleside.com
Opening Hours: 10-11.45 (12.45
Fri & Sat); 11-11.45 Sun

4 Wateredge Inn
Waterhead, Ambleside, LA22 0EP
015394 32332
www.wateredgeinn.co.uk
Opening Hours: 11-11

TRY ALSO:

5 Tweedies Bar
(Dale Lodge Hotel)
Langdale Road, Grasmere,
LA22 9SW
01539 435300
www.tweediesbargrasmere.co.uk
Opening Hours: 12-11 (midnight
Thu-Sun)

Ullswater & the Lowther Valley

WALK INFORMATION

Start/Finish: Pooley Bridge

Access: Bus 108 Penrith to Patterdale via Pooley Bridge

Distance: 9.5 miles (15.4km)

OS map: OS Explorer OL5

Key attractions: Ullswater lake with steamer service; Dalemain House (2 miles); Penrith (4 miles); Clifton Hall pele tower (5 miles)

The pubs: Queen's Head, Askham; Sun Inn, Pooley Bridge

Looking across Ullswater towards Saddleback

Pooley Bridge, lying at the northern end of Ullswater, is a good centre for exploring the north-eastern corner of the national park. There are good walks in all directions: this one takes you onto the open fells of the less-frequented eastern side of the lake before descending into the valley of the Lowther, a tributary of the River Eden. Askham is a pretty village with, typically for the region, a central village green surrounded with solidly attractive houses. Bluebells abound in season in the wooded lower sections of this walk, while higher up, there are expansive views across the lake, the Vale of Eden and across to the highest stretches of the Pennine chain.

One warning: this is the longest walk in the book, although in good weather it shouldn't feel too taxing. Gradients are not demanding and navigation likewise, although you need your wits about you (and preferably a map and compass) descending from Heughscar Hill. For this reason it's probably best avoided if cloud is exceptionally low.

If you're based at Penrith you may be able to arrange a cab to fetch you from Askham which will almost halve the distance.

If you're starting the walk from Pooley Bridge (car drivers can shave about ¾ mile off each end of the walk: see below) walk along the main street past the Sun Inn as far as the parish church and take the turning on the right signposted 'Howtown' then straight across on the 'no-through road' at the next junction which turns out to be a pleasant shady lane with wonderful views across to the lake. At the end of this tarred road, close to Roehead, there is a parking area for car drivers, and a gate leads onto the open commons of Barton and Askham fells.

A wide stony track climbs steadily uphill, the gradient easing after half a mile where you see you're heading for a wide shallow col (or pass) ahead of you. Ullswater Lake is below you, whilst behind, beyond the lake, cloud permitting, Blencathra is distinctive, and from this angle you'll see why it's also known as Saddleback. Ahead, the gently rolling hills and lack of landmarks give a real feeling of big skies and open country.

It's worth making a mental note of both your height relative to the lake and the slight col (pass) ahead of you along this stretch; and the surface of the track. All these will help you be confident on the return later on that you have returned to the correct path when finishing the walk.

As you approach the highest point of this wide track Ullswater disappears and the Pennines come into view. You should be able to spot the distinctive white radar navigation 'golf ball' on the top of Great Dun Fell – Cross Fell, the highest point in the Pennines, is the flat-topped hill to its left.

Passing some clumps of trees close by on the left look out for a standing stone of sorts to the left of the path – here a clear grassy track diverges to the left past the stone, which leads you in three or four minutes to an unfenced road; and if you're at the right spot, a diminutive fingerboard set into the grass points across the road to Setterah Park. Cross the road to continue on the grassy path downhill towards the Lowther valley ahead.

Key

- - - - Walk route

Sun Inn, Pooley Bridge

Ullswater from the bridleway across Askham Fell

Reach a ladder stile ahead of you which marks the edge of the open country. You're just three or four fields away from the village of Helton. The right of way crosses to the bottom left-hand corner of the first long narrow paddock: continue straight down the wall to a gate at the bottom of the next field. 20 yards along an overgrown walled path you'll see a squeezer style on your left. Go through this and walk down to the metal gate you can see at the top of the line of shrubby trees ahead, then it's straightforward: aim for the house with a conservatory in front of you. You'll find a ladder stile, and diagonally beyond this reach the lane at the southern end of Helton. Go straight across onto a signed bridleway marked 'Whale'.

Again this is a stretch which on the ground exceeds expectations – a very agreeable little green lane fringed with trees on both sides, which runs down towards the River Lowther at a wide footbridge in about half a mile. Here, turn back sharply left and follow the river downstream, keeping as close as you can to the river, at one point passing through a shiny new wooden gate before returning to the river bank through some long grass. Then it's a simple walk along the river which then joins a quiet road in about half a mile. Turn right onto the lane and cross the river via the bridge and about 75 yards beyond, a stile by the green and white gate is access to a permitted path across the Lowther Estate.

This path picks up the river again, emptying onto a good stony track running north, with a steep bank of trees between you and the Lowther, and the open limestone fell on your right. You eventually pass through a gate into woodland, 50 yards beyond which take the left fork which drops down

LEFT: **Queen's Head, Askham** RIGHT: **The Punchbowl at Askham: closed, with an uncertain future**

towards the river which at this point is now a faster flowing one along a stretch where wild garlic may fill your nostrils in season. This path will bring you out onto the road at the foot of the village of Askham. Cross the river and pass the church before ascending the hill into the village.

Askham is a delightful place arranged around a long village green. On your left on the way up you'll pass the Punchbowl Inn which at the time of writing is closed and up for sale. If it's re-opened, pop in and try your luck. Continue up the hill to the centre of the village by the crossroads where the **Queen's Head 1** is pleasantly sited and very much open for business. A two-bar pub which retains some character despite modernisation, there's a beer garden, open fires and seats outside at the front of the pub too. Beers are Jennings, Black Sheep and Lancaster Blonde, and you can expect good food and friendly service.

Leaving the Queen's Head, continue in the same direction, still uphill, taking the right-hand of the two no-through roads at the end of which, beyond the upmarket houses with their rather manicured front lawns, go through the gate leading back onto open country. Keep close to the wall on your right (ignore the tarmac path forking left) and let yourself be guided by the wall all the way uphill until you reach a small copse of trees with a gate at the left-hand end of them. Go through here, following the obvious path on the ground which swings around to the right a little, still climbing but quite gently, making for the left end of a long plantation of trees. As you reach the trees you should be able to look back over Penrith, whilst shortly afterwards Ullswater comes into view ahead, away on your left.

Beyond the trees the wide grassy route curves slightly right and leads you towards the summit of flat-topped Heughscar Hill; about 300 yards beyond the tree belt you'll be very close to a small stone cairn just on your right, which marks the technical summit of this flat-topped hill. By all means walk up to 'conquer' the top, but to head down it's the grassy path running downhill from the summit and crossing our current route which we want to take, running down and joining another path running at right angles. Turn right on this path – with luck you'll locate a cairn indicating you're on the right path; here, drop down over the brow and pick your way downhill on a grassy track for some way before rejoining the stony tack near the foot of the slope – the same path we came in on. If in doubt continue downhill until you can see the lane end and car park by the gate at the start of the walk, and remember further up the hill these will be invisible because of the convex shape of the hill.

Once on the right track it's simply a matter of retracing your steps back down to the car park by the gate, and if necessary down the lane back to Pooley Bridge. Either way, by way of reward, make your way to the **Sun Inn 2** on the main street. It's an attractive, busy, Jennings house with their range of beers. There's a large garden for better weather whilst inside a couple of bar rooms and a separate dining area. Food is available lunchtimes and evenings although you might want to phone and check last orders for meals if you look like arriving late. Note that at present the last bus returning to Penrith leaves at 5.36pm.

PUB INFORMATION

1 Queen's Head
Lower Green, Askham, CA10 2PF
01931 712225
www.queensheadaskham.com
Opening Hours: 12–midnight

2 Sun Inn
Pooley Bridge, CA10 2NN
017684 86205
www.suninnpooleybridge.co.uk
Opening Hours: 12–midnight

> **LINK** Bampton (walk 26) is close by, about 4 miles from Askham, but public transport is almost non existent.

High Level Link Route

walk 30: Two classic Lakeland hotels – Langdale to Wasdale

The Old Dungeon Ghyll nestles under the Langdale Pikes

Two classic Lakeland hotels – Langdale to Wasdale

WALK INFORMATION

Start: Old Dungeon Ghyll, Great Langdale (285061)

Finish: Wasdale Head Inn (186087)

Access: Langdale bus 516 to Old Dungeon Ghyll from Ambleside. Very little public transport to Wasdale Head, motor access via Gosforth

Distance: 7.5 miles (12km)

OS map: OS Explorer OL6

Key attractions: The scenery and the beer…

The pubs: Old Dungeon Ghyll, Great Langdale; Wasdale Head Inn, Wasdale Head. Try also: Stickle Barn, Great Langdale

A winter view of Mickleden & Pike O'Stickle

Unlike other routes in this guide, this walk uses a high level path reaching heights of above 2,000 feet to traverse remote mountain country. That said, in good visibility it's a fairly straightforward route navigationally which connects arguably the two classic Lakeland walkers and climbers' hotels: the Wasdale Head Inn – scene of several of the early mountaineering feats and conquests by the pioneers of Lakeland mountaineering – and the Old Dungeon Ghyll. On a good day the route can be accomplished very easily by a fit and experienced hill walker, but it's not your typical pub walk, and you need to be properly equipped for possible conditions at heights of over 2,000 feet. Ensure that as on any mountain walk, you take food and drink – a hot flask is strongly recommended. The rewards, apart from the food and drink at your destination, are some fine mountain views and a definite sense of achievement in crossing the central Lakeland massif in a few hours. The route description given here traverses from east to west but of course it's just as easy to go the other way.

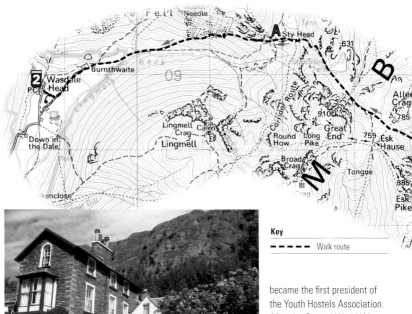

Key

– – – – Walk route

The Old Dungeon Ghyll

A word of warning before you start: In poor weather or where rain and strong winds are forecast this walk is best avoided: it's a long way through what is by English standards a remote area, and you should never underestimate the impact of severe weather, especially if you're inexperienced in fell walking. In particular, the crossing at Esk Hause is notorious in mist and it's all too easy for the inexperienced to lose their way. In these conditions stick to the valley and stay longer in the pubs of Langdale!

Our start point is the **Old Dungeon Ghyll 1** hotel. Steeped in history the ODG, as it's affectionately known, was originally a farm. It had been extended several times so that by the early 1900's when it was sold to the historian Professor G.M. Trevelyan it was known as a hotel. Trevelyan, who was a tireless advocate of historic houses and landscapes, gave it to the National Trust. Incidentally he later

became the first president of the Youth Hostels Association. After the Second World War the cow shed at one end of the building was converted into the climbers' bar, and happily the cow stalls survive to this day. It was frequented by the young postwar climbers like Joe Brown and Don Whillans, whilst climbing clubs from across the land staged events here. The atmospheric bar is just as a pub room in the wilds should be: stone floor, benches, no frills, always characterful. The huge open fireplace is the place to aim for in winter of course. An array of nine handpumps dispensing regulars from Black Sheep, Jennings and Yates alongside a couple of guests ensure that you'll always have plenty of choice. Food is available lunchtimes until 2 and evenings until 9.

The Cumbria Way path skirts the rear of the hotel – to join it, walk down the hotel drive and bear right past Middle Fell Farm to join the wide path (go left to head up the valley at the foot of the slope). Follow signs for 'Mickleden and Rossett Gill'. You're walking up a wide glacial valley with the big hills of the central Lakes away to your left, notably Bowfell, approached by the path up the spur (known as the Band) on the other side of the valley.

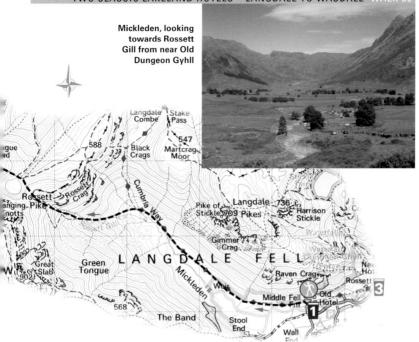

Mickleden, looking towards Rossett Gill from near Old Dungeon Gyhll

Continue on the track, with a wall as your companion for about a mile before you move out across the open valley floor, crossing a minor beck via a stone footbridge and eventually coming alongside Mickleden Beck. Shortly after this you reach the head of the valley where the steep fellsides close in from all sides. Cross Mickleden Beck by a wooden bridge and bear left at a fork, signposted on a slate sign 'Esk Hause'.

The next section of the path, following Rossett Gill is unremittingly steep and pretty rough, the hardest part of the whole route, but at least

View north to Skiddaw and Derwentwater from the path

you won't get lost – it's a well trodden route for walkers accessing the high fells. The other compensation is the opening view, and by the time you reach the point at which the path levels off you'll enjoy, weather permitting, a truly fine prospect back down the length of Great Langdale. Ahead of you there are fine mountain views too, with the glacial corrie lake (or tarn) of Angle Tarn in a depression in front of you, calm and peaceful. This is the obvious first place to take a breather.

There's another climb beyond the tarn – although not as steep or as long as the Rossett Gill slog – which brings you to the col (pass) at Esk Hause, which at about 2,400 feet is by far and away the highest point of any walk in this book, or probably any other pub walks book! On a fine summer's day you'll be happy to stop and enjoy the panorama (although your next pint is still a long way off!); under more normal conditions you'll probably be more inclined to pause briefly for a breather and press on. To your left is the steep buttress of Great End, which marks the northern terminus of the central massif of mountains containing the Scafell range, England's highest. Shortly on your right a path

(which you don't take) heads off along the side of a surprisingly steep cleft occupied by the infant headwaters of what becomes Grains Gill, which runs down Borrowdale and feeds into the River Derwent. On a clear day there's a wonderful view right as far as Skiddaw and Blencathra, the two big mountains on the northern fringe of Lakeland.

Beyond, the path runs gently down to Sprinkling Tarn, still at over 2,000 feet. If temperatures permit this might be a good spot to tuck into your sandwiches. It's not far, but a steady downhill plod, towards Styhead Tarn, where you meet another of the central Lakeland walkers' 'motorways'; that running from Borrowdale (off to your right, northwards) and Wasdale, to the left or south. The view ahead is filled by another of the classic Lake District mountains, Great Gable, just short of 3,000 feet, with the distinctive gap separating it from its smaller neighbour, Green Gable, to the right as you look at it. As you approach with the tarn on your right you'll see the mountain rescue box (A, 218095) adjacent a large boulder – the route you want here heads off to the left close to the box, so head up to the boulder to join the correct path.

Wasdale Head Inn

Walkers at Esk Hause, the highest point of the route

Now, it's again pretty plain sailing as far as navigation is concerned: a short uphill stretch then over a shoulder (it's a bit rocky hereabouts so hands out of pockets!) whereupon the view down into Wasdale suddenly opens out in front- and what a view! At this point the sea should be in view (depending upon visibility) although the famous lake of Wastwater only comes into the view lower down the valley. The white building at the head of the valley is where you're headed for your next beer, so that should renew the weary limbs! The path itself, known as the Moses Trod, is clearly visible as it heads down the valley, so you can enjoy the view as you walk down, re-membering perhaps the man after whom the path was named. The legend goes that one Moses Rigg, a Honister quarryman, had an illicit whisky still on the slopes of Great Gable, and that he conveyed the liquor down to Wadsdale hidden in loads of slate, for like many of today's popular tourist paths, this one originated as a miners' route.

Down below you is the wide flat valley floor at Was-dale Head with its ancient field pattern, and eventually you'll reach it, where just be-yond you'll encounter the first settlement, Burnthwaite, in a lovely setting. Here, as the map shows, the path diverges, both leading to the inn a few hundred yards further on. Take the gate left through the farmyard and then the farm

lane down as far as the little church of St Olaf, a simple building of uncertain age with a roof beam thought to come from a Viking longboat. This is quite plausible since the original inhabitants of Wasdale were certainly of Viking descent. The name of St Olaf though only goes back to 1977 before which the church had no name. It is reported to be the smallest church in England although there are several other claimants… By the church a footpath heads off to the right straight across the final couple of fields to deposit you right outside the **Wasdale Head Inn 2**.

The Wasdale Head Inn describes itself as the home of British climbing, and unlike many of a former landlord's claims (see below) this one has a lot of truth. Many climbing pioneers had their base here, testified by the sepia photographs, some now over a century old, on the walls of the

Langdale Pikes from Hellsgarth

LEFT: **Inside Ritson's Bar, Wasdale Head Inn** RIGHT: **The bar at the Old Dungeon Gyhll**

hotel bar room. The place was originally a farm-house but was enlarged by the legendary landlord Will Ritson in the 1850s to offer accommodation. He had a reputation for tall stories whence the epithet of 'the world's biggest liar' derives, and is the origin of the annual competition.

The entrance to the bar is at the right-hand side of the building: it's a classic walkers' bar with a lovely slate floor, church pew seating and plenty of character. A more comfortable room with photographs leads off the main bar. The Great Gable micro-brewery no longer operates here but the good news is that the array of hand-pumps offers a tempting range of local brews which ought to satisfy a decent session. Food is available throughout the day. Weather permitting, the riverside tables at the rear offer one of the best settings for any alfresco pub drinking in the land. Nearby is the old pack horse bridge which reminds us of the age of the routes which led up to the mountain passes and were used long before the tourists arrived.

The inn offers accommoda-tion (you're well advised to book ahead), whilst there's a small and basic camp site right opposite, and a larger National Trust one a mile down the road.

Tackling the route in the other direction (from Wasdale Head), look for the path to St Olaf's church a few yards up the lane (north of the inn) on the right, then join the bridleway to Burn-thwaite. About a mile up the valley there's a fork of paths – the best option is the left (higher) fork which climbs steadily rather than following the valley floor to the head. The higher path, known as the Moses Trod, leads right up to the mountain rescue box (A, ⊙ 218095) above Styhead Tarn. Here bear right for Sprinkling Tarn and keep to the well-marked path up to and beyond the tarn. At the top of the gorge marked by the head of Grains Gill ignore the prominent path leading off right (this is bound for Great End and the mountains) and instead keep to the path running closer to the stream which leads you up to the col at Esk Hause. Then its pretty plain sailing down the very clear but steep and rough Rossett Gill path to the valley floor of Mickleden, with Great Langdale and the Old Dungeon Ghyll a couple of miles beyond.

If you're game for another beer, the **Stickle Barn 3** is ¾ mile east of the Old Dungeon Ghyll. Beers are from Greene King, Theakston and Jennings plus up to two changing guests from local micros, and there's a pleasant garden.

PUB INFORMATION

1 **Old Dungeon Ghyll**
Great Langdale, LA22 9JY
015394 37272
www.odg.co.uk
Opening Hours: 11-11
(10.30 Sun)

2 **Wasdale Head Inn**
Wasdale Head, CA20 1EX
019467 26229
www.wasdale.com
Opening Hours: 11-11; 12-10.30 Sun

TRY ALSO:

3 **Stickle Barn**
Great Langdale, LA22 9JU
015394 37356
Opening Hours: 11-11;
12.10.30 Sun)

Accommodation

THE WEST:

Eskdale

Boot Inn
www.bootinn.co.uk
Brook House Inn
www.brookhouseinn.co.uk
Bower House Inn
www.bowerhouseinn.co.uk
King George IV
www.kinggeorge-eskdale.co.uk
Woolpack Inn
www.woolpack.co.uk

Nether Wasdale

Screes
www.thescrees.co.uk
Strands Hotel
www.strandshotel.com

Ravenglass

Holly House
rachelfrangy@yahoo.co.uk
Pennington Hotel
www.penningtonhotels.com

Seathwaite

Newfield Inn
www.newfieldinn.co.uk

Waberthwaite

Brown Cow
www.thebrowncowinn.com

Wasdale

Wasdale Hall
www.yha.org.uk

Wasdale Head

Wasdale Head Inn
www.wasdale.com

THE SOUTH WEST:

Barngates

Drunken Duck
www.drunkenduckinn.co.uk

Bowmanstead

Ship
www.shipinn.info

Broughton in Furness

Black Cock
www.blackcockinncumbria.com
Manor Arms
www.manorarmsthesquare.co.uk
Old Kings Head
www.oldkingshead.co.uk
Manor Arms
www.manorarmsthesquare.co.uk

Coniston

Black Bull
www.blackbullconiston.co.uk
Sun
www.thesunconiston.com

Elterwater

Britannia Inn
www.britinn.net

Far Sawrey

Sawrey Hotel
www.sawrey-hotel.co.uk

Foxfield

Prince of Wales
www.princeofwalesfoxfield.co.uk

Great Langdale

Langdale Hotel
www.langdale.co.uk

Old Dungeon Ghyll
www.odg.co.uk

Hawkshead

King's Head
www.kingsarmshawkshead.co.uk

Little Langdale

Three Shires Inn
www.threeshiresinn.co.uk

Near Sawrey

Tower Bank Arms
www.towerbankarms.co.uk

Skelwith Bridge

Skelwith Bridge Hotel
www.skelwithbridgehotel.co.uk

Torver

Church House Inn
www.churchhouseinntorver.com

Ulverston

Bay Horse Hotel
www.thebayhorsehotel.co.uk
Farmers Arms
www.thefarmers-ulverston.co.uk
Stan Laurel Inn
www.thestanlaurel.co.uk

THE SOUTH EAST:

Allithwaite

The Pheasant Inn
www.the-pheasant.co.uk

Cartmel

Royal Oak
www.royaloakcartmel.co.uk

Great Strickland

Strickland Arms
www.thestricklandarms.co.uk

Ings

Watermill Inn
www.watermillinn.co.uk

Kendal

Riverside Hotel
www.riversidekendal.co.uk

Kirkby Lonsdale

Orange Tree
www.theorangetreehotel.co.uk
Plato's
www.platoskirkbylonsdale.co.uk
Sun
www.sun-inn.info

Staveley

Eagle & Child
www.eaglechildinn.co.uk

Brook House Inn, Eskdale

Troutbeck

Mortal Man
www.themortalman.co.uk

THE NORTH WEST:

Braithwaite

Coledale Inn
www.coledale-inn.co.uk
Middle Ruddings Country Inn
www.middle-ruddings.co.uk

Buttermere

Bridge Hotel
www.bridge-hotel.com
Fish Inn
www.fishhotel.com

Loweswater

Kirkstile Inn
www.kirkstile.com

Portinscale

Derwent Lodge
www.derwentlodgehotel.co.uk

Rosthwaite

Scafell Hotel
www.scafell.co.uk

THE EAST:

Ambleside

Queen's Hotel
www.queenshotelambleside.com
Wateredge Inn
www.wateredgeinn.co.uk

Askham

Queen's Head
www.queensheadaskham.com

Bampton

Mardale Inn
www.mardaleinn.co.uk

Bampton Grange

Crown & Mitre
www.crownandmitre.com

Caldbeck

Oddfellows Arms
www.oddfellows-caldbeck.co.uk

Grasmere

Dale Lodge Hotel
www.tweediesbargrasmere.co.uk

Pooley Bridge

Sun Inn
www.suninnpooleybridge.co.uk

Rydal

Glen Rothay Hotel
www.theglenrothay.co.uk

Shap

Greyhound
www.greyhoundshap.co.uk

Lake District transport

Getting there:

The Lake District has a long tradition of being a rural retreat for walkers and holidaymakers. Trains on the West Coast mainline connect Oxenholme, Penrith and Carlisle, from where you can connect to local trains, with London and Glasgow. Driving is always an option, and it may make sense to choose a hub to base your Lake District holiday from, and leave your car there. Any of towns in the Lake District would make a good base for easy access to transport and amenities, but if you want a more relaxed rural retreat, many of the pubs on the routes offer accommodation options. The accommodation index (p153) provides region-by-region listings and contact details

National travel info:
nationalrail.co.uk, 08457 484950
nationalexpress.com

Getting around:

Towns and villages such as Ambleside, Windermere, Coniston and Keswick are linked by bus,

with extra services in the summer. There is also a train line following the Cumbrian coastline. You will need either a car, careful planning or stout walking boots to reach some of the remoter areas. Drivers should take extra care as even A roads can be winding and some of the mountain passes traverse the steepest roads in England. Walking link routes can be found on pages 32, 40 and 147-52.

Local travel info:
nationalrail.co.uk, 08457 484950
nationalexpress.com

Local bus operators:

Almost all of the walks are accessible by public transport. Where there is a useful bus route, it is listed at the start of the walk in the route information box. Bus services are provided by either the County Council or commercial service operators (principally Stagecoach). Information about their timetables can be found on cumbria.gov.uk, stagecoachbus.com, or by calling Traveline.

Places index

Pubs index

Beer index

Newfield Inn, Seathwaite

CAMPAIGN
FOR
REAL ALE

Books for beer lovers

CAMRA Books, the publishing arm of the Campaign for Real Ale, is the leading publisher of books on beer and pubs. Key titles include:

Good Beer Guide 2011

Editor: Roger Protz

The *Good Beer Guide* is the only guide you will ever need to find the right pint, in the right place, every time. It's the original and best-selling guide to around 4,500 pubs throughout the UK. Now in its 38th year, this annual publication is a comprehensive and informative guide to the best real ale pubs in the UK, researched and written exclusively by CAMRA members and fully updated every year.

£15.99   ISBN 978-1-85249-272-5

Edinburgh Pub Walks

Bob Steel

A practical, pocket-sized traveller's guide to the pubs in and around Scotland's capital city. Featuring 25 town, park and costal walks, Edinburgh Pub Walks enables you to explore the many faces of the city, while never straying too far from a decent pint. Featuring walks in the heart of Edinburgh, as well as routes through its historic suburbs and nearby towns.

£9.99   ISBN 978-1-85249-274-8

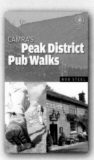

Peak District Pub Walks

Bob Steel

A practical, pocket-sized traveller's guide to some of the best pubs and best walking in the Peak District. This book features 25 walks, as well as cycle routes and local attractions, helping you see the best of Britain's oldest national park while never straying too far from a decent pint. Each route has been selected for its inspiring landscape, historical interest and welcoming pubs.

£9.99   ISBN 978-1-85249-246-5

BOOKS

Order these and other CAMRA books online at
www.camra.org.uk/books,
ask at your local bookstore, or contact:
CAMRA, 230 Hatfield Road,
St Albans, AL1 4LW. Telephone 01727 867201

CONISTON BREWING Co.

Premium
XB
*Bluebird
Bitter*

TRADITIONAL HAND BREWED
CASK CONDITIONED

CBC

USING ONLY THE FINEST
SELECTION OF HOPS & MALTS

Oliver's
light Ale

CBC

3.4% Vol.

USING ONLY THE
SELECTION OF HOPS

*Bluebird
Bitter*

CBC

3.6% Vol.

USING ONLY THE FINEST
SELECTION OF HOPS & MALTS

*Old Man
Ale*

TRADITIONAL HAND BREWED
CASK AND BOTTLE CONDITIONED

CBC

ABV 4.4% Vol.

USING ONLY THE FIN
SELECTION OF HOPS

*Special
Oatmeal Stout*

DITIONAL HAND BREWED
CASK CONDITIONED

CBC

ABV 4.5% Vol.

USING ONLY THE FINEST
SELECTION OF HOPS & MALTS

WINTER WARMER
*Blacksmiths
Ale*

TIONAL HAND BREWED
BOTTLE CONDITIONED

CBC

USING ONLY THE FINE
SELECTION OF HOPS &

*Consistently
Good Beer*

Coppermines Road, Coniston
Cumbria LA21 8HL
Tel: 015394 41133 Fax: 015394 41177
www.conistonbrewery.com sales@conistonbrewery.com

It takes all sorts to Campaign for Real Ale

CAMRA, the Campaign for Real Ale, is an independent not-for-profit, volunteer-led consumer group. We promote good-quality real ale and pubs as well as lobbying government to champion drinkers' rights and protect local pubs as centres of community life.

CAMRA has 115,000 members from all ages and backgrounds, brought together by a common belief in the issues that CAMRA deals with and their love of good quality British beer and cider. For just £20 a year — that's less than a pint a month — you can join CAMRA and enjoy the following benefits:

A monthly colour newspaper and quarterly magazine informing you about beer and pub news and detailing beer festivals around the country.

Free or reduced entry to over 140 national, regional and local beer festivals.

Money off many of our publications including the *Good Beer Guide* and the *Good Bottled Beer Guide*.

Access to a members-only section of our national website, **www.camra.org.uk** which gives up-to-the-minute news stories and includes a special offer section with regular features.

The opportunity to campaign to save pubs under threat of closure, for pubs to be open when people want to drink and a reduction in beer duty that will help Britain's brewing industry survive.

Log onto **www.camra.org.uk** for CAMRA membership information and how to join.

CAMPAIGN
FOR
REAL ALE